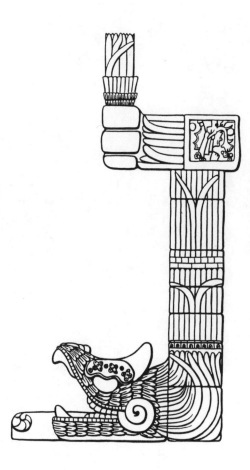

THE
YUCATAN

A GUIDE TO
THE LAND OF
MAYA MYSTERIES

by Antoinette May

Wide World Publishing/ Tetra

Acknowledgements: This book owes much to the moral and practical assistance of Ruth Shari of Mexicana Airlines, the photography of C.J. Marrow and Vern Appleby, the knowledge of Joan Hallifax, Peter Balin, Brother John and Lola of the Ojai Foundation, the enthusiasm of Ann Shotland and–most specially–to Ann Axtell Morris who provided the spark.

front cover photograph: Chichen Itza by C.J. Marrow
back cover photograph: author at Tulum

Pagination is reflected in Mayan numerals as well as the conventional numeration.

Design and graphics by Theoni Pappas

Wide World Publishing/Tetra
P.O. Box 476
San Carlos, CA 94070

Second printing 1988.
Printed in the United States of America.

ISBN: 0-933174-43-8
Library of Congress Catalog Card Number: 86-051427

For Vern—
a tigre on the trail and
everywhere a consummate trouble shooter

CONTENTS

Columns at Chichen Itza

Introduction

"There was nothing standing;
Only the calm water, the placid seas,
alone and tranquil.
Nothing existed.

"Then they planned the creation,
And the growth of trees and thickets
and the birth of life.

"Thus let it be done!
Let the emptiness be filled!
Let the water recede and make a void.
Let the earth appear and become solid;
Let it be done, thus they spoke.
Let there be light, let there be dawn in the sky and
on the earth!

Popol Vuh

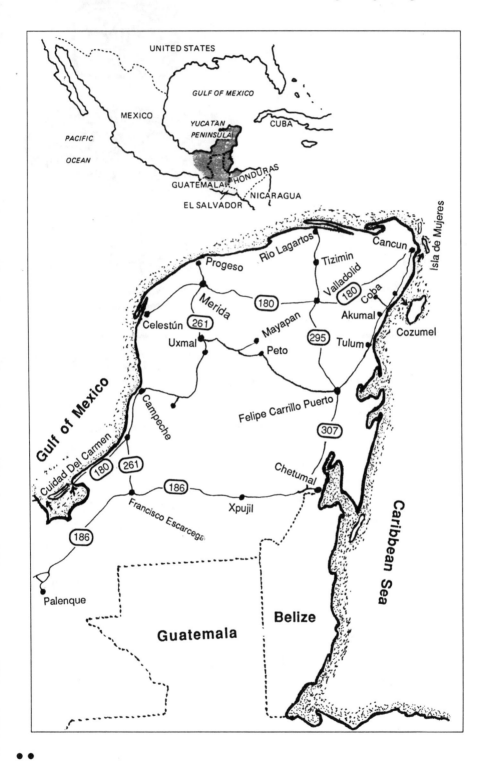

When Atlantis sank, Yucatan rose–and that's just one story. The mysterious Maya have inspired many.

Though the Aztec and Inca civilizations were the dominant ones at the time of the Spaniards arrival, it's the world of the ancient Maya that appeals most to the imagination. All we really know is that the Mayan empire, consisting of more than 100 city states, flourished for a millennium. During their ascendency these mysterious people formulated the concept of the zero before the Arabs and devised a calendar more accurate than the one we use today. Then, as mysteriously as it all began, the Mayan civilization abruptly ended.

The Mayas built great cities, abandoned them, then returned hundreds of years later. Why?   Some of their toys had wheels and yet they didn't make use of this basic tool in their labors.   Why did this seemingly simple connection elude them?

When the first Europeans set foot on the ancient soil of the "New" World, most of the Mayan ceremonial centers had been gobbled up by jungle. Only the tallest buildings still towered above the dense vegetation. Who built these cities only to desert them? they asked, as we do today.

Devout Christians that they were, the Spaniards believed that every human was descended from not just Adam and Eve but Noah and his family, the sole survivors of the great flood. But how could the Indians of the new world claim such descent? Since they couldn't, it meant the Maya Indians weren't quite human.   That rationalization helped the conquistadores to justify a lot.   Who would blame them for killing or enslaving animals?

The "animals" had to be protected from themselves.   One of

● ● ●

the most vicious of the protectors was Diego de Landa, first bishop of Yucatan, whose auto-da-fe was intended to–and perhaps did–wipe out the entire Mayan history. In his eyes the manuscripts consigned to the flames contained "nothing but superstition and falsehoods of the devil."

Eventually even the conquistadores complained about the extent of de Landa's missionary fervor. The priest was recalled to Spain and imprisoned. With time on his hands, de Landa did an amazing thing. He attempted to replace what he'd destroyed by compiling an account of everything he'd observed about the Mayas at the time of the conquest and every story he'd since heard about them.   That record, lost and then found 300 years later, constitutes the bulk of what little we know today about the Mayan civilization.

While languishing in prison, Landa recalled a story told to him by an old man who said that his ancestors believed themselves descended from a race that had come from the east by way of twelve paths opened through the sea for them by God. From this legend, Landa hypothesized that the Mayas must be descended from one of the Lost Tribes of Israel. He was eventually freed and his theory gained popularity throughout the 16th and 17th centuries.   It still has proponents which include The New World Archaeological Foundation funded by the Morman church.

As they learned more about the magnificence of the Mayan civilization, Europeans simply could not believe these amazing people weren't a transplant from their own world or at least a world with which they were familiar. As a result, the Maya Indians were from time to time identified as descendants of Norse explorers, Phoenician traders, shipwrecked Huns, Romans, Africans, Irishmen, and even crew members from the lost fleet of Alexander the Great–or even Alexander himself.

• • • •

A theory dating from the 16th century which is frequently reintroduced is that the Mayas are refugees from the lost continent of Atlantis. According to legend, Atlantis was a great island in the Atlantic that was destroyed by volcanic eruptions, earthquakes and tidal waves. Unproven and frequently derided, the story of this sunken continent lying buried beneath the sea is a myth that refuses to die. It's estimated that some 3000 books have been written about Atlantis in the last 2500 years. If the physical reality remains to be established, the significance of the myth's psychological reality can't be disputed.

Many believe that this lost continent is the ancestral home of both the Egyptians and the Mayas. A leading proponent of this theory was the French Abbe Charles Etienne Brasseur de Bourbourg, who became an expert on the Mayan language. This brilliant 19th century scholar was responsible for saving many early colonial manuscripts from destruction when the monastic orders were finally suppressed—among them Bishop Landa's lost manuscript. He translated the *Popol Vuh,* the Mayan bible, and other ancient writings, then climaxed a lifetime of research by publishing his premise that the civilizations of Egypt and the Old World came from the New World, where they had previously been brought by colonists from Atlantis.

Augustus Le Plongeon, an archeologist and physician, shared his beliefs. Le Plongeon and his wife, Alice, began their excavation of Chichen Itza in the midst of a minor revolution, settling into a fortified church and walking three miles each day to the ruins. A precursor of Carlos Castaneda, Le Plongeon won the confidence of the Indians who confided to him ancient secrets jealously guarded from the Spanish, secrets for which their ancestors had been tortured or murdered.

Le Plongeon described these revelations as having "a rich living current of occult wisdom and practice, with its sources in an extremely ancient past, far beyond the purview of ordinary historical research." Occasionally, he believed, the mask was lowered sufficiently for him to glimpse "a world of spiritual reality, sometimes of indescribable beauty, again of inexpressible horror."

Some of this was revealed in his book, *Queen Moo and the Egyptian Sphinx,* which draws frequent parallels between the Egyptians and the Mayas. Both civilizations had pyramids, hieroglyphic writing, relief sculpture and many common words. The controversy that Le Plongeon unleashed more than 100 years ago continues to this day.

Serpent scultpure at Chichen Itza

The most popular theory today is that the Mayas–like all the Indians of the Americas–migrated from Asia over a long period of years via a land bridge that once spanned the Bering Strait. But if this one seems too ho-hum, consider the most recent hypothesis: extra terrestrials. The much discussed "Mayan obsession with time" takes on new meaning to some who speculate that the early Mayas were explorers or refugees from another planet, people desperately calculating just how long their supplies would last. These same theorists insist that there must be some reason why both the United States and Russia are spending millions of dollars each year on Mayan research.

Far out? Literally and assuredly, yet a sarcophagus at Palenque does resemble a man at the controls of a spacecraft. There is an astronaut *look* about the ubiquitous Descending God. The debate seems likely to stretch into infinity itself.

The best known of all the 19th century explorers fascinated by the Maya mystery was John Lloyd Stephens The fact that Stephens, a prominent New York attorney, had helped to elect President Martin Van Buren didn't hurt a bit when he asked for the position of U.S. Diplomatic Agent to the government of Central America.It was hoped the title might come in handy should an insurrection occur—which it did more than once.

His companion on the journey was the English born artist, Frederick Catherwood who'd traveled and painted extensively in the Near East. Catherwood's fascination with old ruins and exotic cultures was extreme. In order to gain admission to the mosque of Omar where he wished to make detailed architectural drawings, he submitted himself to circumcision.

Undeterred by the grudging welcome they received from the war torn population, Stephens worked for months uncovering the ruins while Catherwood struggled to capture them with pen and ink. Groggy from malaria, their bodies swollen from insect bites, they continued their work until Catherwood collapsed.

••

When Stephens and Catherwood finally staggered out of the jungle they had the makings of what would be one of the great best sellers of their century. *Incidents of Travel in Central America, Chiapas and Yucatan,* a two-volume book, *revealed* a whole new world to the general public and introduced a word that had not appeared in any dictionary. It was Maya. Within three months the book went through ten printings.   When Catherwood regained his health, the two returned. The result of the second trip, *Incidents of Travel in Yucatan,* another two volume tome, was an even better seller.

Stephens and Catherwood explored the Yucatan Peninsula nearly 150 years ago hacking their way through almost impenetrable jungle. "We sat down on the very edge of the wall, and strove in vain to fathom the mystery by which we were surrounded," Stephens wrote in 1840. Today, with all our modern innovations and conveniences, the mystery remains the same. Again and again, we ask as he did:"Who were the people who built these cities?"

And, again like Stephens, we attempt to solve the puzzle, pondering: "In the ruined cities of Egypt, even in the long-lost Petra, the stranger knows the story of the people whose vestiges he finds around him.   America, say historians, was peopled by savages; but savages never carved these stones."

Again, like Stephens, we seek answers from the descendants of the Indians who excavated these abandoned masterpieces. Their answer is invariably the same:
"Quien sabe?"

• • •

Catherwood's drawing of the Governor's Palace at Uxmal

Sketch of the Temple of the Magician at Uxmal by Frederick Catherwood

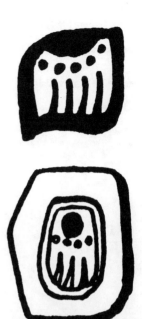

Romancing the Ruins

"...without the wheel, draft animals or metal cutting tools, Mayan engineers, artisans and laborers built magnificent cities."

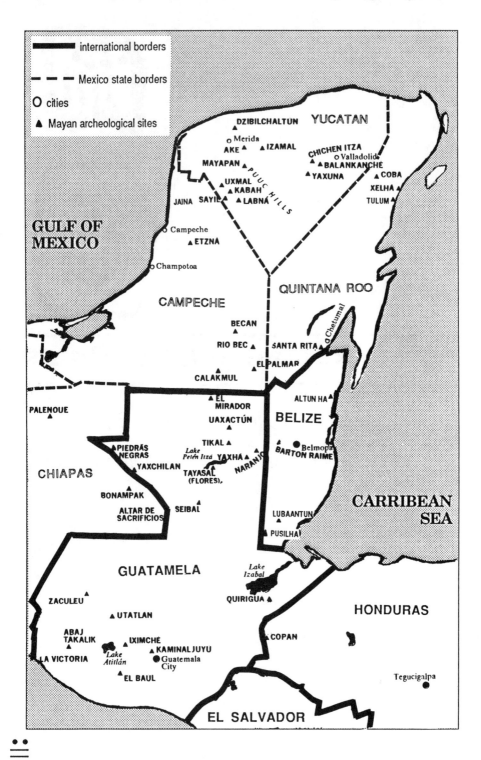

international borders
Mexico state borders
O cities
▲ Mayan archeological sites

YUCATAN

DZIBILCHALTUN
o Merida
AKE ▲   ▲ IZAMAL
MAYAPAN   CHICHEN ITZA
        o Valladolid
        ▲ ▲ BALANKANCHE
UXMAL   ▲ YAXUNA   ▲ COBA
▲ KABAH   XELHA ▲
JAINA SAYIL ▲ LABNÁ   TULUM ▲
PUUC HILLS

GULF OF
MEXICO
        o Campeche
        ▲ ETZNA

        o Champotoa

CAMPECHE   QUINTANA ROO

        BECAN ▲   o Chetumal

        RIO BEC ▲   SANTA RITA ▲
            EL PALMAR ▲
        ▲
    CALAKMUL   ALTUN HA ▲

PALENQUE   ▲ EL   BELIZE
▲   MIRADOR
        UAXACTÚN ▲

            TIKAL ▲
        Lake
    ▲PIEDRAS   Petén Itzá YAXHA ▲   ▲ Belmopan
    NEGRAS   NARANJO   BARTON RAIME
CHIAPAS   ▲ YAXCHILAN
            TAYASAL
    ▲   (FLORES)
    BONAMPAK   CARRIBEAN
    ▲   LUBAANTUN   SEA
    ALTAR DE   SEIBAL ▲
    SACRIFICIOS
            PUSILHA ▲

    GUATAMELA   Lake
                Izabal
                QUIRIGUA ▲
    ZACULEU ▲   HONDURAS

    ▲ UTATLAN
    ABAJ
    TAKALIK   IXIMCHE   ▲ COPAN
    ▲   ▲ KAMINALJUYU
    LA VICTORIA   Lake   ● Guatemala
        Atitlán   City   Tegucigalpa ●
        ▲ EL BAUL

        EL SALVADOR

A ny "lost" civilization will inspire a sense of mystery as one ponders the fate of ancient cities covered over by greedy jungles. But an even greater puzzle than the cause of the Mayan decline is the question: how did this civilization ever exist in the first place? And, then, by implication, how could it have lasted as long as it did? Most specifically, how it could have existed where it did?

How could the level of social and political organization needed to sustain this civilization be attained in areas of impassable forests, rank vegetation and dangerous animals? Yet it was in just such places that the Mayan culture reached its highest level. In many areas the ground is nothing more than porous limestone, the topsoil seldom more than a few inches deep. What little water there is collects in channels below the ground and runs into the sea without ever coming to the surface. How could the greatest civilization in the Western Hemisphere have developed in this hostile environment?

What we know is merely that it did. We also know that without the wheel, draft animals or metal cutting tools, Mayan engineers, artisans and laborers built magnificent cities. Around 1500 B.C., the Mayas are believed to have migrated from Central America into Yucatan, an area described by de Landa as "the country with least earth that I have ever seen, since all of it is one living rock and wonderfully little earth."

Why did they abandon a hospitable environment to begin anew in such a hostile one? No one knows.

We do know that this was the beginning of the **Preclassic Period** which continued until approximately 300 A.D. Bows and arrows yet to be invented, the Mayas hunted with snares and spears. They were considerate hunters killing only what was needed. This is still true. Respect for the dignity of the animal and gratitude for its ultimate gift, is demonstrated by the modern Mayan hunter when he explains to the animal he has killed, "I have need."

The slash and burn method of agriculture which requires great experience on the farmer's part evolved from this early time and is still in use. A patch of forest is selected and cut down in the late autumn. Then at the end of the dry season the brush is burned. The maize seed is poked into the ash with a stick. This milpa has a lifespan of only two years. Then the farmer must abandon it for 15 to 20 years and go to another area of the forest and begin again. The everyday life of the Preclassic Maya centered around the rain, sun and wind gods who were–and still are–evoked when the fields are cut, burned and planted, and when the crops are growing.

Then in 500 B.C.– at the same time the ancient Greek civilization was flourish-ing–the Mayas began to make great strides. Centuries before the birth of

The Maya zero symbol

Christ, the Mayas developed what has been called "one of the brilliant achievements of the human mind," a system of numeration by position involving the concept and use of the zero.

This is all the more striking when compared with the clumsy Roman numerical system used in Europe at that time where the zero was unknown. Why should an agricultural people living in the midst of a jungle bother with such a highly sophisticated mathematical system? But

---

[1] Although the Babylonians are credited with the earliest development of a positional number system, this does not diminish the achievement of the Mayas.

• • • •
══════

would the Mayas have invented such a complex order if they hadn't had　use for it? What was that use? These seemingly primitive people measured time in units larger than 23,000,000,000 days.　One can only marvel and wonder once again:　why?

In the next 800 years–while Jesus was born, preached and was crucified, Jerusalem was destroyed and the Jewish Diaspora took place, and the Roman Empire climbed to its zenith and waned–the Mayas were developing their calendar–more accurate than the Gregorian calendar introduced in 582 A.D., their beautiful and highly complex hieroglyphic writing, and their architecture.

Then in 300 A.D., while the barbarians were sacking Rome and the Dark Ages were spreading over Europe, the Mayas made a quantum leap into their Golden Age.　What we know today as the **Classic Period** must have been grounded in a kind of spiritual awakening. Some mysterious, invigorating impulse instilled in the Mayas a profound sense of the transitory nature of life.　One response was an urgent need to make some kind of enduring mark, another was to record the passage of worldly events.

Nineteen major cities–that we know of–were built at this time along with countless minor ones.　Clay mounds gave way to colossal pyramids of cut stone, majestic temples and palaces adorned with intricately carved facades and exqui- site sculpture. The style was remarkably sophisticated, as introspective as that of Asia and as naturalistic as sculp- ture found in the Mediterranean areas. Mayan artists achieved a three dimensional effect by foreshortening when they chose, but for the most part preferred a flat, painterly approach.　The effect of so much baroque ornamentation is one of order in complexity. The rigid formality of earlier monuments gave way to a dynamic imbalance within different parts of the composition which continues to fascinate while leading the eye restlessly along.

Stelae–great stone monuments–an example of early day public relations celebrating the personal triumphs and grand activities of kings and city states, were commissioned by rulers everywhere. Korbeled arches, solar observatories, water reservoirs, all the practical applications of an advanced civilization, appeared.

The finest examples of Mayan architecture were conceived and constructed at this time, long before the Gothic style appeared in Europe. How was the creation of these grand cities possible for people without wheels, metal cutting tools or dray animals? How did they transport the giant stones for their temples and pyramids when there was no stone in the area itself? How did they manage to move huge stone heads weighing twenty tons or more through miles of jungle?

The mysteries don't stop here. We know but two things about the Classic Mayan civilization. It evolved and then ended. All the rest is pure conjecture. By 900 the Golden Age was over. The sad story is revealed by what wasn't said. One means of measuring time was in batkuns. No commemorative stelae record the opening of Batkun 10 in the ninth century of our era.

What came next is known as the **Postclassic Period.** Almost over night it seems many of the great ceremonial centers had been abandoned.   An epidemic, perhaps?   A revolution? Famine? Earthquake?   No record or historical indication has ever been found pointing too any of these possibilities. Whatever happened, we know that a few isolated groups stayed on, camping out in the rooms of forgotten palaces–much like the Lancandon Mayas do

Rendition of the Mayan bas-relief of the jaguar at Chichen Itza.

today—burning copal incense before the likenesses of mortal men who slowly evolved into gods.

Then, in the llth century, about the time the Normans were conquering England, the Toltecs conquered the Mayas. These grim militarists from central Mexico were a new order of men replacing the intellectual leaders of Classic times. The conquest was brutal and violent in the extreme. Warrior gods were introduced, blood sacrifices accelerated. But, like many conquerors, the Toltecs were absorbed by their new subjects, becoming essentially latter day Mayas.

There were many wars before the big one with the conquistadores and even that was not final. There were also many more cities built, some we have yet to find. In 1840 John Stephens wrote of a city hidden deep in the jungle where chickens were kept underground to prevent anyone from hearing them crow and and where the Mayas killed any intruder unlucky enough to happen upon them. Such hidden cities are being discovered to this day, and each time are found to be deserted. How long have they been that way?

Verdant jungle growth

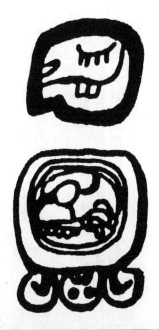

Who's Who of the Gods

Existence depended on a multitude of sacred beings who controlled the universe and everything in it. The cosmos was neutral; its mighty forces neither good nor bad–merely capricious. Like the gods of ancient Greece and Rome, the Mayan deities were often childlike creatures subject to fearful tantrums. Because they were dependent on human attention for their welfare, they could be manipulated.

From Palenque–the lid of a sarcophagus depicting the venerated ceiba tree, and other objects , such as the two headed sky dragon and celectrial birds

T he lush, green Mayan cosmos was centered around a giant ceiba tree. Its sacred foliage reached into the heavens, the thrusting roots twisted deep into the underworld. The precious ceiba was the vortex of a kind of compass, each direction having its own colors. The north was white, the south yellow, the east red and the west black. These four directions were the keys to an understanding of religion and magical thinking.

But there was an even more important part to the compass. It was the center. This was the place where man was at any given moment. It stretched as far up as the eye could see as well as deep into the underworld. Its color was green, the green of jade, the most precious of Mayan minerals.

Each day the sun began its celestial journey through this cosmos, beginning in the east and climbing into a heaven—arranged in thirteen layers like a pyramid—until it reached the west where it slowly began its descent into the nine layers of the dreaded underworld. The sun's sacred passage through the sky and into the underworld was also symbolic of human life for it is in just this way that man rises, becomes vigorous, weakens and dies.

Life was a dicey business for the Mayas, highly transient in contrast with the permanence of the world about them. Existence depended on a multitude of sacred beings who controlled the universe and everything in it. The cosmos was neutral; its mighty forces neither good nor bad—merely capricious. Like the gods of ancient Greece and Rome, the Mayan deities were often childlike creatures subject to fearful tantrums. Because they were dependent on human attention for their welfare, they could be manipulated.

Kind, cruel, capricious—the gods of the Maya were just like

•
•
•

their human worshippers, in turn bitter, sweet or blankly indifferent. It was dangerous to ignore such moody, frivolous beings, creatures jealous of their power and prominence who constantly expected to be worshipped, celebrated or placated. They had to be housed and cared for, diverted with music and dance and–most importantly–fed.

Each deity could have two aspects or twenty, might appear magnanimous to some, avaricious to others. A single god s duties and attributes could vary according to his mood or the circumstances. Not only could the Mayan gods change their function and nature, they could also change form. The same deity might appear as young or old and sometimes even changed sex. Frequently they were known by different names in different circumstances.

In time of drought, Chac, the rain god, would be viewed as aloof or neglectful, withholding his favors for reasons of forgetfulness or even anger; but during periods of abundant rain, he was thought benevolent and generous. In war time, the same god or goddess might be simultaneously regarded as rewarding or punishing–since a victory for one is invariably a defeat for others.

In other words, the triumphs and failures, harvests and famines, victories or defeats of the Mayas were directly related to the trenchant moods of some basic personalities. In so much as a "who's who" can be compiled of such chameleons, here it is:

Hunab Ku–the greatest god, the creator of the world, father of the divinities, the one god alive and true, and the deity responsible for the flood that destroyed the four worlds that proceeded that of the Mayas. This was the supreme god, but beyond shape and substance so that he could never be represented pictorially.

Itzamna–(Hunab Ku's son)–the sky god, was –for the most part– a benevolent being very like Jupiter in that he presided over the day and the night, and was the sage of all the gods. It was Itzamna who first invented calendars and taught the priests to write. The patron of wisdom and learning, Itzamna–from whom the Itza tribe believed themselves sprung–is depicted as a toothless old man with sunken cheeks, a thin beard and a hooked nose.

Ixchel–(Itzamna's wife) –goddess of the moon, prophesy, childbirth, procreation, medicine, shells, and weaving. Though these are associations involving the concept of renewal, Ixchel is frequently portrayed as a capricious crone with a headdress of entwined snakes, a necklace of bones, and jaguar-claw fingernails.

Chac–the rain god, is also the overlord of the gods of the wind who ruled the four corners of the world and held up the sky. Chac controls thunder and lightning and is often attended by toads who serve as his minstrels. In a largely agrarian economy, his

. . .

importance remains considerable. Months without rain go a long way to explain Chac's survival to this day. His image is ubiquitous in Mayan architecture, reaching out from countless friezes everywhere In what appears to be a conscious effort to instill terror, he is invariably portrayed with huge, empty eye-sockets and what looks more like an elephant's trunk than a nose.

Kukulcan–the fabled plumed serpent is the deity of healing and magical herbs, the lord of hope and the morning star, a

god of spring-time and emergent life. The major symbol is a serpent wearing the gorgeous feathers of the quetzal bird, but sometimes he's shown as a man wearing a special loincloth with a rounded end, apparently a bag to hold his oversize penis. Though celibate, he was viewed as the fertilizing breath of life. His story is the eternal one of sin and redemption, death and resurrection, the transfiguration of man into god. Somehow through the alchemy of time, he changed into a rapacious taskmaster who demanded blood sacrifices in return for the sun's fertilizing rays.

Ek Chuah–both a war god and a protector of merchants and travelers. As the war god, he's depicted with a black body holding a spear. In that dark, shadow form, Ek Chuah was feared as a fire-raiser and a destroyer of homes; but he was also venerated as the lord of the cocoa plant whose

beans were used as money. In the latter guise, he was considered the protector of merchants who prayed to him before setting out on their journeys. In this capacity, he's shown as a merchant with a pack on his shoulders.

Ah Xoc Kin–god of the sun, was the inventor and patron of both poetry and music. His glyph resembles a St. Andrew's cross which he's generally pictured wearing on his clothing or forehead.

Ah Puch–lord of death and the underworld is beyond question the most terrible god in the Mayan pantheon. Not only does he lie in wait for men and hinder plant growth, he actively hinders fertility. Ah Puch is usually depicted as a skeleton or a death's head.

Ixtab–goddess of suicide, is seen hanging by her neck. She was considered very important, as it was often necessary to atone to the gods for wrong doing. Suicide was considered a form of ritual cleansing like hari kari. It was through Ixtab's assistance that those who took their own lives were able to find their way to a special paradise in heaven.

Yum Kaax-the handsome, young maize god, personified the ideal of male beauty. He protected not only the maize shoots but young married couples. Yum Kaax is depicted with a headdress of leafy plants and feathers. Maize has always been considered the greatest gift of the gods and is itself venerated. Some present day Mayas still address it as "Your Grace." In ancient times a period of abstinence was observed during the planting season and offerings were made in the fields. The Mayas never went to war during planting season, maize came before everything.

Xaman Ek-god of the North Star, was particularly important to traders and mariners and assisted architects with the alignment of their buildings. He is portrayed with black flecks and a snub nose.

Chac-Mool-the messenger of the gods. The hearts of sacrificial victims were often placed in basins held by stone replicas of this demi-god.

Are the old gods dead? Not likely. The Lacandon Mayas, who live in remote areas, have never accepted Christianity and even in "civilized" areas one finds recent traces of candles and incense before ancient shrines. Shamen using sacred chants and crystals are still sought for their spells and healing techniques. Secret societies continue to exist.

In the four centuries since Catholicism was forcibly introduced, many of the gods have taken on saintly overtones. As an example, the Virgin Mary has fused for many with Ixchel. Kukulcan, wearing a mask and plumed headdress, sometimes replaces Santa Claus at holiday parties or in store windows, once again bringing life and gifts of happiness to the people. Like it or not, the padres admit that the deities of ancient days remain much in evidence.

It can be said that the Mayas also worshipped time and cycles of time. The first world cycle was thought to have been destroyed by jaguars representing the earth, the second cycle by air, the third by fire, the fourth by water, a great flood. The fifth cycle, in which we are currently living, is predestined to be destroyed by earthquake.

The Mayas believed that this present cycle began in the year 13.0.0.0.0. 4 Ahau 8 Cumku (their calendar) or August 12, 3113 B.C. The ending was predicted for December 24, 2011.

The Mayan cyclical pattern is based on multiples of 52. At the end of this Calendar Round cycle (when the solar year and the sacred year calendars coincide), the people extinguished all their fires, lamented and fasted, believing that the world might be destroyed. The end of two of these cycles every 102 years—when solar, sacred and Venus calendars converged—assumed even greater significance.

Of the end of the Great Cycle of 5,200 years there was no doubt. A catastrophe would completely destroy the world as it had on four previous cycles. The duration of these five worlds was thought to total 26,000 years which very closely approximates the known 25,920-year cycle of the precession of the equinoxes.

The Plumed Serpent – Chichen Itza

The Plumed Serpent

"The human embodiment of divine love and wisdom as well as an able administrator, he united the people and ruled them under one large confederation of tribal groups."

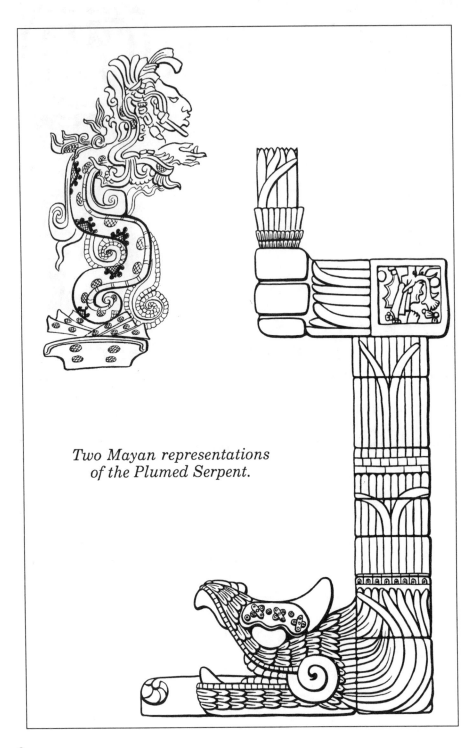

*Two Mayan representations
of the Plumed Serpent.*

T he fabled Kukulcan reaches out to us across the century—a figure of romance, betrayal, illusion and eternal mystery. *Who* was he? *What* was he?

Known in other parts of Mexico as Quetzalcoatl, Kukulcan appears much like King Arthur, half man, half myth. Little is known, much is conjectured; and the facts themselves merely add to the puzzle. According to the story, Kukulcan descended from heaven and preceded to introduce the concepts of penitence, love and exemption from the traditional rituals of blood sacrifice. The human embodiment of divine love and wisdom as well as an able administrator, he united the people and ruled them under one large confederation of tribal groups.

As with the Arthurian Round Table, it was all too good to last. The high priests and warriors didn't take kindly to Kukulcan's substitution of incense, flowers and maize for human sacrifices. There had to be a way of removing him......and, of course, eventually they found it.

Kukulcan was known to be vigorous, sexually potent, and endowed with an enormous penis; yet he vowed to remain celibate, sublimating his considerable energies in good works. Finally the day came— naturally it would have to be a ceremonial day with an attendant cast of thousands— when the wily priests handed Kukulcan a drink laced with magic mushrooms. While under the influence of this powerful aphrodisiac, he was tempted by a beautiful woman and made love to her.

Awakening later, he was consumed with guilt. In his own eyes Kukulcan had condemned himself by breaking his self imposed vows. Leaving behind everything— palaces, kingdom, clothes—he arrived naked on the shores of the Caribbean. After promising to return one day, Kukulcan embarked on a raft of snake skins and sailed eastward until a tremendous heat ignited the boat and, in a burst of flames, his heart arose, flying upward to finally merge with the sun.

Kukulcan's spring time promise is familiar to mythmakers everywhere. He is the martyr who must inevitably suffer, then be driven away or killed before he can return to the kingdom of heaven—and ultimately be born again. This time the self sacrificing god returns as the Morning Star, a symbol of hope and regeneration.

Fact or fantasy? The glyphs in the Vienna Codex record this spectacular astral happening as a solar eclipse, an event verified by the Royal Observatory at Greenwich as having occurred on July 16, AD 750.

The story of Kukulcan's disappearance was told and retold. It was a legend that refused to die, for everyone knew that just as the god had been overthrown in the past, so he would one day return to overthrow his adversaries and usher in a new era of peace and justice. The hope remained for hundreds of years until the early 16th century when history and mythology united to produce a great tragedy.

Stone serpent looking out from deep undergrowth at Chichen Itza

Gateway at Labna by Catherwood

The Way It Was

"Ci-u-than," their shouted reply, meant simply, "We don't understand you," but the Spaniards believed the words to be the answer to their question. Somehow Ciuthan evolved into Yucatan. Years later a conquistador attempted to set the record straight when he wrote that the Mayas "now say their country is called 'Yucatan,' and so it has that name, but in their own language they do not call it by that name." Unfortunately, he neglected to mention exactly what they did call it and now no one knows.

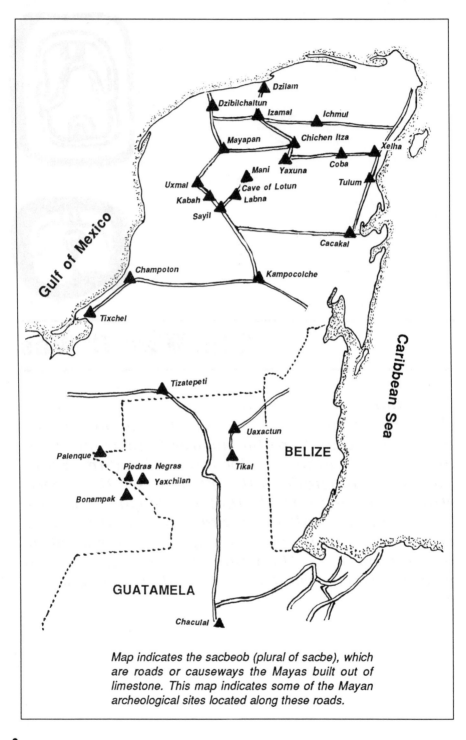

Map indicates the sacbeob (plural of sacbe), which are roads or causeways the Mayas built out of limestone. This map indicates some of the Mayan archeological sites located along these roads.

"**W**e don't understaaaaaand yoooooooooou!"

The words echo eerily down through the centuries. Perhaps this initial communication breakdown explains why the old world believes it not only discovered the new, but invented it as well.

The Spanish explorers studied these new Indians as though taking inventory: strong noses flared slightly at the nostrils, straight black hair, eyes like shining jet buttons under ridged brows, thick, full lips. But there was something else, something more. These mysterious strangers possessed an air of confidence and quiet dignity.

The Indian trading party was leaving now, getting back into an immense dugout canoe. "What do you call yourselves?" the Spanish commander called after the departing boat.

"Ci-u-than," their shouted reply, meant simply, "We don't understand you," but the Spaniards believed the words to be the answer to their question. Somehow Ciuthan evolved into Yucatan.   Years later a conquistador attempted to set the record straight when he wrote that the Mayas "now say their country is called 'Yucatan,' and so it has that name, but in their own language they do not call it by that name." Unfortunately, he neglected to mention exactly what they did call it and now no one knows.

The Mayas, too, were bewildered by the encounter. What manner of thing was this white-winged floating tower? And who were these tall, ungainly men with their white, hairy faces? Before long word of the meeting had spread across the country all the way to Montezuma in the far northwest.

What would follow was unique in the long, cruel chronicle

of exploration and conquest. Two entirely separate worlds were about to collide. Each possessed equally long records of achievement, yet both had been totally oblivious to the existence of the other.

A sense of fate overshadows much of Mexican history. Poor, frightened Montezuma had been waiting for the shoe to drop for several years. From his palace rooftop, the ruler who'd once been a priest searched the skies for portents each day at dawn, sunset and midnight. In 1508 he'd watched with apprehension as a tiny black speck crossed the face of the sun. The last time the planet Venus had transited the sun had been 300 years before. A devastating flood had followed. Now he felt certain that some similar disaster was pending.

When the first man, a lowly peasant, came to him with a strange tale about "a small mountain floating in the midst of the water, moving here and there without touching the shore,"   Montezuma closed his ears to the account. The trouble maker was thrown into prison for spreading such ridiculous lies. But then messengers arrived from the king of Tulum, deep in the Maya country to the southeast, confirming the report. Two great mountains or towers were, indeed, floating in the sea. Worse yet, they contained tall, light skinned beings with beards and hair that came only to their ears. Montezuma lowered his head.

Quetzalcoatl

For a time he said nothing as thoughts of the Quetzalcoatl legend returned to plague him. Was the god not tall, fair, bearded?

Quetzalcoatl's return had long been foretold. He'd promised to appear before them again in some Ce Acatl year on the day of his birth, Chiconaui Ehecatl. This combination, which came up every 52 years, was scheduled to occur in the spring of 1519—only a few months away.

In Cuba, Hernando Cortes had never heard of Ce Acatl but hoped that the year 1519 would bring something more rewarding than a job running a small plantation where the Carib Indians had to be watched every minute. (The damn fools would rather commit suicide than work for a Spaniard.) A short, ordinary looking man who walked with a permanent limp since falling from his mistress's balcony, Cortes had big ideas. Even he couldn't have imagined himself as a god incarnate and yet destiny had drafted him for that role.

The 34-year-old adventurer was intrigued by tales of land to the west. Even if there was no gold— as had been rumored— there was at least a native population to enslave. He hoped they'd prove a more tractable bunch than the Caribs. The Governor of Cuba mounted an expedition but was delayed. There was some last minute finagling and Cortes took his place. In the governor's eyes it was to be merely a reconnaissance mission; Cortes envisioned it quite differently.

Meanwhile in Montezuma's palace a great sadness had overtaken the court. The ruler's beloved aunt, Princess Butterfly, fell ill and died. Then three days later the noblewoman astonished everyone by sitting straight up on her bier.

The joy that Montezuma felt at her miraculous recovery was quickly shattered. In what appears to have been an out-of-body experience, Princess Butterfly had seen men wearing black stones and riding hornless deer. She went on to describe the capital city in flames, her nephew's murder and the subsequent reign of the most dreadful of the white-faced creatures.

Only a short while later Montezuma received word that men of her description had disembarked from a "winged tower that floated across the sea." The date was April 21, 1519. The Spaniards called it Good Friday, but Montezuma knew that it was Chiconaui Ehecatl, the birthday of Quetzalcoatl in the year called Ce Acatl.

He considered his doom sealed. Who could fight a god? This sense of grim inevitability explains the takeover of a mighty nation by only a few men. By the time that Montezuma realized that they *were* merely men, it was too late.

It was an initial encounter with the Mayas that first stimulated the Spaniards to launch an extensive mission to Mexico; but, for a time, Yucatan was bypassed by the conquistadores.

Cortes didn't get around to dispatching a force to subdue the area until 1527. Then Francisco de Montejo was granted the title, *adelantado* , with permission to exploit Yucatan at his own expense. It's curious to note that the Mayas–the first to make contact with the Spaniards–were the least in awe of them.

Perhaps because they'd had ample opportunity to intimately

study two shipwrecked Spanish sailors, the Mayas had no illusions that their would-be conquerers were gods. They didn't have to fight fate–just men, superior weapons, and smallpox. It took four tries and more than 20 years before the Spaniards succeeded in conquering them–in contrast with two years to completely subdue the Aztecs.

Montejo longed to give up completely. Deeply discouraged, he wrote to the king, *"In these provinces there is not a single river, although there are lakes, and the hills are of live rock, dry and waterless. The entire land is covered by thick bush and is so stony that there is not a single square foot of soil. The inhabitants are the most abandoned and treacherous in all the lands discovered to this time. . ."*

Despite the fact that the Mayas were divided into numerous autonomous provinces, often at war with each other, they still resisted fiercely. Worse yet–from Montejo's point of view–they refused to stay conquered. He lost his entire fortune trying to subjugate the Mayas, finally turning the whole venture over to his son.

Spurred on by priests who weren't about to relinquish their power easily, the rebellious Mayas planned a massive counter attack for the night of the full moon on November 8, 1546–5 Cimi, 19 Xul, in the Mayan calendar, a date designated in their sacred almanac as " Death and the End."

For them, it was the end.   But, though the conquest of Yucatan was considered complete by 1547, it continued in a low-key, sporadic way for the next 150 years. The Spaniards actually lost ground as they were forced from time to time to pull back.   The Mayas, too, pulled back, forming refugee settlements deep in the interior. The Lacandon Mayas were never conquered and remain unchanged to this day.

At first the Mayas cyclical view of time helped to facilitate the transition. There's comfort to be found in a world in which history and prophesy intertwine in recurring patterns, events repeating themselves in the same orderly fashion as planets.   "This too shall pass," they believed. All things, both good and bad, have their appointed times to end–if only so that they may be repeated later.

While the conquistadores searched fruitlessly for gold, the missionaries were determined to transform the Mayas into idealized Spanish peasants. Here at last was raw material with which to work, subjects that could be molded into standards of sobriety, thrift, industry and propriety unrealized anywhere else.

 The resulting introduction of Christianity into Yucatan produced a far more serious crisis in the Mayan world than the devastation of military warfare and political domination.   Nothing in their history of conquests could have prepared the Mayas for the Spaniard's determination to obliterate their entire culture, but at first they scarcely realized what was happening.

There was nothing unusual about a victorious army introducing a new god. It had happened many times. Not only was it prudent to accept the new pantheon of personalities forced on them, but desirable.   The superior military strength of the Spaniards was reason enough for the pantheistic Mayas to recognize that the new Spanish religion was a force to be reckoned with.

The child Jesus was appealing enough, the Mother Mary vaguely reminiscent of Ixchel. The sticking point was the jealous nature of the head god. Accepting this new personage as a sacred being was not the same as accepting him as the *only* sacred being in the cosmos. The idea that

: :

divinity was concentrated in this one remote figure to the exclusion of all the more familiar and intimate deities that permeated their world was incomprehensible to the Mayas. The friars could forbid the new converts to worship their old deities but convincing them that such veneration was futile or unnecessary was another matter. The Mayas believed that a sacred umbilical cord linked heaven and earth. Nourishment flowed in both directions sustaining men and gods. A ban on ritual could cut this essential cord placing the entire cosmos in jeopardy.

The culture shock that resulted from this assault on the whole nature of the Mayan universe is difficult to imagine. Too soon the once willing converts discovered that the missionaries who'd so patiently explained the exemplary qualities of their god could be as cruel and implacable as the soldiers.

Devotions to the old gods were severely punished. The lightest sentence was 100 lashes and interrogation techniques were brutal. The good friars had brought with them from Spain all the refinements of the Inquisition. Many Mayas died or were crippled for life. (In a single day, Sebastian Vazquez, His Majesty's Clerk in Merida, recorded that 4,549 men and women were hanged and tortured by the monks.) Others—in the words of the padres— "displayed their cowardice" by committing suicide before the questioning could be completed.

Fray Diego de Landa was the worst of these zealots. In 1552, while serving as Franciscan Provincial, Landa may have forever destroyed the key to Mayan civilization by burning every hieroglyphic record he could find along with hundreds of statues, stelae and altar stones. As a result, until fairly recently, all that we know about the Mayas at the time of the conquest or a thousand years before has been filtered through the writings of those appalling padres. Since most of the Spanish priests shared the view of the conquistadores that the Mayas were "beasts" or "natural slaves," very little survived.

Eventually the Mayas embraced certain aspects of Spanish culture. They built Spanish style houses–though many confessed to finding them less comfortable and healthful than their former ones. They adopted the heavy breeches and tunics, capes, cumbersome shoes and plumed hats, which proved even more unsuitable to the climate. Not surprisingly, they took to swords with far more enthusiasm and discovered a true affinity to European wines and spirits.

The uneasy dominion over the Mayas was to last for nearly 300 years; and the ending, when it came, was rooted in events far away. The wars of independence that overthrew the Spanish Empire in America grew out of Napoleon's occupation of Madrid and the subsequent collapse of Spanish power. Self government was at last literally thrust upon the Creoles, and the taste for it spread from liberals to conservatives, who together achieved independence in 1821.

Because of its isolation, Yucatan had always been controlled directly from Spain rather than Mexico City. Now for a brief glorious period Yucatan was once again autonomous.

In 1823, the Yucatan Peninsula joined with Mexico. It was an uneasy partnership that would explode in less than twenty years. Meanwhile, the peninsula was a caldron of discontent. One of the chief causes was the change in landholding practices accelerated by independence. With the large scale introduction of sugar cane and henequen cultivation, vast haciendas or landed estates evolved, feudal empires each employing hundreds of Mayas who were tricked into virtual slavery.

The hacendados, or land owners, who took pride in their direct lineage back to the conquistadores, realized that the only way to keep the Mayas down on the farm was to entice them into debt. When this method didn't net a large enough labor force, a new state constitution was passed in 1825 compelling the Indians who couldn't pay taxes in money to pay them in work. The hacendados and their puppet politicians agreed that once the Indians owed money, they must be kept owing until they were so deeply mired that they could never buy their way out.

The world was rapidly changing and Yucatan with it. The United States and Europe needed rope for shipping. Here was a handy source of supply. The hacendados discovered wealth beyond their avaricious dreams. Ignoring the rest of Mexico as not worth bothering with, they turned to Europe for cultural standards. Children were educated on the Continent and while the Mayas worked the land, the hacendados partied in Paris. A way of life was developing, a nobility of style as well as birth that required that one's wealth be produced by the labor of the lower orders. It would cost the landed Creoles dearly.

In 1838 civil war broke out between the liberal federalists who desired more autonomy for the provinces and conservatives who wanted a strong government in Mexico City. It was to culminate in the disastrous war between Mexico and the United States in 1846. When Yucatan seceded from Mexico, the same Mayas who provided virtual slave labor to the hacienda owners were drafted into the army. From the Creole point of view, it was a very foolish mistake.

Having been issued arms in order to defend independent Yucatan from Mexico and the United States, the Mayas instead turned those guns on their local oppressors. On July 30, 1847 the "War of the Castes" was launched. Valladolid, the most isolated and vulnerable of the Yucatan cities–and the stronghold of the most arrogant Creoles– soon fell to the Maya forces. Next Merida was threatened. Appeals for help to Spain, the United States and France went unanswered. Then, just as the governor was preparing to evacuate Merida, the Mayas picked up their weapons and walked away.

Vengeance was sweet but corn was the heart's blood of the Maya. When the rains come, the corn must be in the soil. The victorious Mayan soldiers turned their backs on certain victory and returned to their fields.

This was just the respite the Creoles needed. Help came at last from Cuba, then the United States sent 1000 "military advisors." Reprisals were merciless. Mayan men, women and children were slaughtered whatever their economic or political beliefs. Others were sold to Cuba as slaves. The lucky ones escaped into the jungles of Quintana Roo which remained a literal no-man's land for nearly 100 years. An estimated 300,000 people–half the population of Yucatan– were killed in the war which wasn't over yet.

What the Mayas needed was a rallying point and one day it miraculously appeared. It began with a poor, peasant who happened on to a sparkling spring. Water had always been hallowed by his people, so the man carved three crosses on a sacred ceiba tree growing closeby. From ancient times the cross had held a special significance for the Mayas who saw it as a kind of divine compass.

Gradually word spread that the crosses had come down from heaven in order to make sacred revelations to the fighting Mayas. When the crosses suddenly began to speak, a cult sprang up. Of course the voice was generally conceded to be that of a ventriloquist, but there was a precedent for that going back to an oracle on the holy island of Cozumel. People came from all around and built houses near the spring. Their settlement became the village of Chan Santa Cruz; and they, themselves, were known as the *Cruzob* , or People of the Cross.

It was believed that the words of the cross were divinely inspired. The message was a rallying cry to the Mayan soldiers who were back from their planting and ready to go again. After a series of successful skirmishes, the Mayas achieved a *de facto* independence and were recognized by the British who were delighted to sell arms in exchange for timber. Until the end of the 19th century a shaky truce prevailed. The *Cruzobs* and their talking crosses ruled the southern Caribbean coast, an isolated jungle kingdom now theirs by default.

Meanwhile, in the northern peninsula the hacendados continued to grow richer and richer while their Mayan peasants barely survived. The haughty Creoles had changed little. So anxious were they to establish their superiority by setting themselves apart that they passed a law decreeing that women of mixed blood were required to wear *huipals*, Indian dresses. Augustus Le Plongeon, an archeologist excavating in Chichen Itza during the 1870's, reported that working men on the haciendas were pitilessly and arbitrarily flogged by their overseers, then put in stocks overnight so as not to miss a day's work. Were they, he wrote, to lay their grievances before the owner of the hacienda, their only redress was to receive a double beating for daring to complain. "If they lodged a complaint before a judge as by law they had the right, he is the friend or relative of the planter. He may himself be a planter. On his own plantation he has servants who are treated in a like manner."

It was more than forty years before a new type of politician arose. Felipe Carrillo Puerto was a brave and charismatic leader who gained the support of the peasants and some-how rose to the governorship of Yucatan.   Once in power, Puerto organized labor unions and educational centers, then decreed that haciendas not in use be appropriated for the Mayas who had once owned all the land.

The growing power of this upstart who refused to see which side his political bread was buttered on was too much for the reigning Creoles. The man had to be stopped and he was. In 1924 Felipe Carrillo Puerto was assassinated along with every male member of his family that could be found.

What was meant to be an object lesson came too late. The winds of change were blowing. A series of sweeping re-forms instituted in Mexico City helped to liberalize the so-cial and economic life of Yucatan. President Lazaro Carde-nas (1934-40) broke up many of the hacendados and distrib-uted parcels to small farmers. In 1936, Cardenas gave half of Quintana Roo, then still a territory to the poor. He also signed a treaty with the still active descendants of the *Cru-zobs* thereby finally putting an end to the conquest of the Mayas.

And today? It's a cruel fact of life that Mexico's economic and political burdens are a boon to the tourist and the out-side investor. In 1976 the inflation that was effecting the world was literally pricing Mexico out of the market. In an attempt to remedy this critical situation, the peso was allowed to float, finding its own value against the dollar. Response to this legislation brought foreign capital back in a hurry. It's hoped that the influx will create enough jobs to correct the economic condition.

Cancun

Sunset view at Cancun

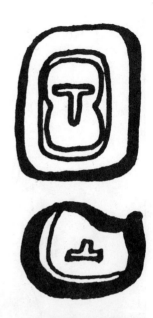

Cancun
(kahn-koon)

"Like the mist, like a cloud,
And like a cloud of dust was the creation,
When the mountains appeared from the water,
And instantly the mountains grew."
Popol Vuh

And the keys clicked, the data banks gave forth
their sacred information and the
Great Computer spake:
"BUILD THE CITY HERE."

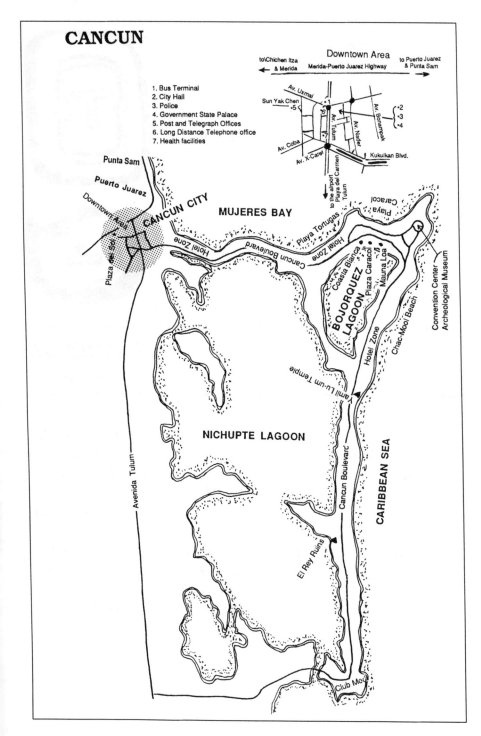

CANCUN

Downtown Area

to\Chichen Itza & Merida   Merida-Puerto Juarez Highway   to Puerto Juarez & Punta Sam

1. Bus Terminal
2. City Hall
3. Police
4. Government State Palace
5. Post and Telegraph Offices
6. Long Distance Telephone office
7. Health facilities

Av. Uxmal
Sun Yak Chen
Av. Coba
Av. X-Caret
Av. Tulum
Av. Napel
Av. Bonampak
Kukulkan Blvd.
to the airport
Playa del Carmen
Tulum

Punta Sam
Puerto Juarez
Downtown Area
CANCUN CITY
Plaza del Sol
MUJERES BAY
Hotel Zone
Cancun Boulevard
Playa Tortugas
Playa Caracol
Convention Center
Archeological Museum
BOJORQUEZ LAGOON
Coasta Blanca
Plaza Caracol
Mauna Loa
Hotel Zone
Chac-Mool Beach
Yamil Lu-um Temple

NICHUPTE LAGOON

Avenida Tulum
Cancun Boulevard
El Rey Ruins
CARIBBEAN SEA
Club Med

T he posh, polished resort of Cancun may be the only island in the world to be "discovered" by electronic technology. When the Mexican government sought to create a state of the art tourist mecca in 1967, it collected every scrap of information about what tourists want. When processed by computer, the result was Cancun.

The Popol Vuh, the Mayan book of creation, says that only by a miracle, only by magic art were the mountains and valleys formed. Then instantly the groves of cypress and pines put forth shoots together on the surface of the earth. Almost as suddenly a vacation paradise emerged seemingly overnight from a tropical wilderness once the domain of macaws and spider monkeys.

It began in 1970 with a small task force. The island had to be connected to the mainland and widened, in some places, it was too narrow to even accommodate a coastal road. Since the area was virtually uninhabited, *chicleteros* were recruited to work on the project. It was a whole new world for these brave men who'd spent most of their lives deep in the neighboring jungles harvesting gum from the *chicle* tree.

Communication was the next problem, for the workers spoke only Mayan and the architects, engineers and planners only Spanish. Three years later the international airport was completed, but there were no lodgings for guests until 1974. Today there are 6000 hotel rooms and a whole network of services to amuse and bemuse the visitor.

The spawn of Mother Nature and Father Computer is still an infant seeking an identity. People will love or hate it according to their tastes. By Mexican standards Cancun is pricey, but compared to the United States, it remains relatively reasonable. Too young for tradition, too raw for distinction, the city none-the-less strives for elegance and sometimes achieves it. Hotels range from comfortable to ultra luxurious. Restaurants offer something for every appetite: Cajon, Parisian, Hawaiian, Italian and mucho Middle American.

Hyatt Caribbe – Cancun

Where is Mexico one wonders after passing the fifth pizza parlor, the tenth hamburger palace? Well, there is still an area that remains pure Mexico. The toilet is the same sacred well frequently rejecting our sacrifices. Mexican plumbing retains its independent spirit even here.

Cancun is not a shopper's paradise. Prices are often twice as high as in areas only a few miles away. Worse yet, the wares are, for the most part, a ho-hum assortment of trivia. Despite the prices there's a border town feeling. Merchandise is trucked in from all parts of the country and plunked down. "Okay, Gringos, this is an authentic piece of Mexico–grab it." Unless you literally fall in love with an object or don't plan to continue on into other parts of Mexico, you're better off to wait.

But what does Cancun offer?

• *Climate*– warm, balmy, an average of 80 degrees, 240-plus days of sunshine every year. (Miami has only 93.)

• *Ambience*– the sea's incredibly blue, the sand like talcum powder and so white that it reflects the sun's heat remaining comfortably cool to the touch.

• *Accessibility*– one of the closest foreign destinations within a few hours of any major North American city.

There are quickie bus tours to the ruins of Tulum and Chichen Itza, party cruises, scuba diving, wind surfing, deep-sea fishing. If this is your first trip to Mexico, you'll find comfort in menus printed in English, water you can drink from the tap and the sense that you and your money are very much desired.

But others will see Cancun primarily as a point of departure, the first hint of more exciting things to come. Across the blue lagoon from the glossy hotels and sleek condos, the mysterious jungle beckons.

GETTING AROUND

Shaped like an art nouveau seahorse–or more prosaically a "7"–the island of Cancun is almost fourteen miles long and a quarter of a mile wide. It's bounded by lagoon on one side and the Caribbean on the other and attached to the mainland by two bridges.

Kukulkan Boulevard runs the length of the island and connects all the hotels and beaches there with Cancun City. A public bus system services the entire area on a regular basis at a nominal fee. Taxis from mainland to island are surprisingly reasonable, but it's wise to avoid occasional unpleasant exchanges by establishing the price in advance.

If you're in Cancun for more than a weekend, I can't recommend strongly enough that you rent a car or jeep and get out into the countryside. It's practically impossible to get lost either in town or on the highways–there are so few of the latter. Tulum is very close, Coba and Chichen Itza not so very much farther. Along the way there are fascinating villages and exquisite beaches to explore.

Car rental agencies are abundant, competitive and offer any number of package deals. Maps are readily available and the roads are excellent–but it is important to start off with a full tank, for gas stations aren't as prevalent in Mexico as they are at home.

All the tour buses make a point of visiting Tulum in the morning and Xel-ha in the afternoon. Your enjoyment of both would be enhanced 100 percent if you reversed that order thereby escaping the madding crowd.

WHERE TO STAY

Cancun has two hotel areas: the fancy one on Cancun Island with prices to match and the more moderately priced Cancun City. The so-called "hotel zone" is on the island. Here all have their own beaches, one or more restaurants, bars, shops, pools and often travel agencies.

Personal favorites among these class act operations are:

Exelaris Hyatt Cancun Caribe– A replica of Chac-Mool gazes out to sea here–like any other sunbather. And why not? This may be the best beach in town. All 202 rooms in the crescent shaped high rise have a view of the Caribbean on one side, the lagoon on the other.

Cancun Sheraton Resort– This one has it all–including its very own Mayan ruin. Discovered in 1842 by John L. Stephens and Frederick Catherwood, Yamil Lu'um was once a temple and navigational outlook. The highest natural point on the island, it looms large above sun worshippers lounging on the beach below.

Camino Real– The vaguely Mayan slope-sided architecture is beyond the last word. Beside it stands a small shrine believed to have been an offertory to the sea. The grounds also include beachfront, a fresh-water pool and a private salt-water lagoon.

Krystal Cancun– No ruins here, but the Krystal is home to two of Cancun's most popular attractions, ***Bogart's Casablanca*** and the lively disco, ***Christine.***

Exelaris Hyatt Regency –Where the action is – within easy walking distance to the Convention Center, archeological museum and the largest concentration of shops, restaurants and nightclubs. When your feet give out, the inner courtyard with its hanging gardens of Babylon architecture is ideal for people-watching.

CANCUN CITY

The Parador Hotel is modern, comfortable and well located with a refreshing oasis-like feeling about the pretty courtyard and pool area.

Hotel America and *Hotel Plaza del Sol* operate their own shuttle vans to private beach clubs and marinas.

All combine the standard amenities with convenient downtown shopping and kind to the pocketbook prices.

WHERE TO EAT

Cancun is seafood heaven. Lobster, shrimp and a variety of fish are fresh and good here; but since this is a city created for tourists, one needn't be limited to Neptune's garden. Whatever your preference, it's readily available with some innovative nods to current fads and fancies.

When in Cancun, I do as the Cancunians do—eat Cajun. The best in town is found at the *Blue Bayou* in the Hyatt Caribe. The "blackened" lobster is divine and with it one of the great soups of the world, cream of artichoke with oysters. A special treat is the "Sexy Coffee" after dinner—a warm and sensuous blend of everything imaginable flamed at your table. An orchestra plays for dancing, the service is impeccable.

Yes, it's expensive, but worth it.

At the other end of the spectrum pricewise is **Restaurantes Los Almandros** at Avenue Bonampak in Cancun City. Here's one of those rare things in Cancun – an authentic Mexican restaurant. If you want typical Mayan fare in a reassuringly santitized atmosphere, this is the place.

The building approximates a mammoth Mayan palapa, the background music is lively but not too loud, the glassed in kitchen immaculate. A colorful menu shows pictures of the native specialties with explanations in English. Two of us spent less than $10 for a dinner that included *sopa de lima* (lime and chicken soup), *poc-chuc* (broiled pork meat with tomato, onion, coriander and oranges) served with black beans and tortillas plus three bottles of Carta Blanca.

Shrimp with Schubert? Veal with Vivaldi? Pasta with Puccini? The classical background music at **Chac-Mool** (next to the Aristos Hotel in the Chac-Mool Beach complex) is particularly impressive combined with the crashing surf outside. The food and service stand up well to comparison.

The Bombay Bicycle Club advertises a "great piece of tail." They refer to lobster, of course, and also guarantee the best ribs since Adam's. It's that kind of place–silly and sensational – with charcoal-grilled lobster, chicken, burgers, pizzas, fried bananas. Fresh squeezed orange juice and chocolate croissants are a breakfast specialty which returnees to Cancun have made a tradition.

Bogie would probably have loved **Bogart's,** everyone else does. This well appointed restaurant in the Krystal Hotel is awash with nostalgia. Happily, the place fulfills its promise. Excellent international cuisine, attentive service and relatively reasonable prices.

WHAT TO DO

• *SHOPPING POSSIBILITIES*

Two good ones in the El Parian Commercial Center next to the Convention Center are *Victor* which specializes in high grade Mexican arts and crafts and *Anakena* which features original paintings, Mayan temple rubbings and hand engraved shells.

At *Artland* in the Terramar Shopping Center across from the Fiesta American Hotel, one can find an exciting selection of silk screen work, art prints, black coral jewelry, ironwork, wood carvings and silver.

The Costa Blanca Shopping Center in the newly created Zona Rosa has two specialty shops well worth checking out. *La Iguana* is a mad menagerie of creatures made from papier-mache or brass and copper. *Mayart* offers reproductions of museum sculpture plus carved masks and temple rubbings.

In most shops prices are established, but bargaining is practiced at the booths at the Ki-Huic market downtown and Coral Negro by the Convention Center. Store hours are usually from 9 or 10 a.m. to 1 p.m. and from 4 or 5 p.m. to 9 p.m.

Products most native to the area are the *huipil,* a straight muumuu style dress with rich embroidery around the hem and neckline, and hammocks, hats and handbags made from henequen. Despite the abundance of tortoise shell jewelry for sale, this is a no-no with U.S. Customs. The turtle is on the endangered species list.

In less than twenty years a tiny village has grown to a city of 120,000 inhabitants whose round the clock efforts insure a happy holiday.

•*ARCHAEOLOGICAL SITES*

Quintana Roo was the home of the ancient Maya, one of the first shores touched by the Spanish conquistadors and a refuge for marauding pirates. To get a sense of this rich cultural history, a visit to the Museo Arqueologica de Cancun is a must. The small but well appointed museum is located next to the Convention Center near Punta Cancun. The hours are from 10 a.m. to 5 p.m. Tuesday through Saturday. Admission is nominal.

El Rey Ruins were named for the skeleton found on top of the pyramid. Archaeologists speculated that he might have been a king since there were other human remains found at the base of the structure. This was a small ceremonial

Yamil-Lu'um, ruins at Sheraton Hotel

center for Mayan fishermen, built very early, then abandoned and resettled near the end of the Postclassic Period, not long before the arrival of the conquistadors. On the west (the lagoon) side of the road, this site is marked by a small wooden sign at the entrance. A dirt road leads to the site which borders the lagoon. Admission is free.

Pok-Ta-Pok was discovered by workmen constructing the 12th hole of the Robert Trent Jones Golf Course. This small ruin from the Postclassic Period is well preserved.

•*ON THE SEA*

If you've always wanted to learn or perfect a water sport, Cancun is tailor-made. The clear, year-round warm waters afford perfect conditions. Most hotels have centers where windsurfers, sailboats, kayaks, scuba and snorkeling equipment may be rented and English-speaking instructors are on hand to give fast and easy lessons to those who need them. There's also a wide selection of deep-sea fishing opportunities.

If you like party cruises, the Fiesta Maya is available to take you on a five-hour trip to Isla Mujeres. Pirates brandishing swords leap down on unsuspecting passengers for souvenir photos and voluptuous volunteers are selected to mimic the sacrificial rituals in which the hearts of victims were removed. There's an open bar, dancing, loud music and a host who works so hard making it "fun" that some would gladly pay him to take a siesta. Many others obviously enjoy this cruise and find it an easy, effortless way to see Isla Mujeres as well as the lagoon and mangrove swamps. (Another possibility is the ferry which bypasses the swamps but also the noise.)

•NIGHT LIFE

Variety is the spice of Cancun. Every hotel on the island offers its own brand of entertainment ranging from jazz combos to specially arranged "fiestas." My personal favorites run the gamut.

The Ballet Folklorico is a dinner show rather than a ballet in the theater sense. The evening begins at 7 with an enormous buffet supper possibly weighted more to quantity than quality but there's certainly plenty from which to select. At 8:30 the performance begins. Though not yet the equivalent of the Mexico City extravaganza, the thirty dancers and musicians are *good* . Two evenings before I'd seen a roadshow production of *Cats* in San Francisco. It seemed a walk through in contrast to this lively, well executed performance. The whole event – food, entertainment, service – works well. Shows are staged in the **Convention Center** auditorium nightly except Sunday.

Wednesday is nostalgia night in the romantic Atrium Park Lobby of the **Exelaris Hyatt Regency.** *Moonlight Serenade* is a sentimental journey into the 20's, 30's and 40's. A champagne dinner is served from 6:30 to 10:30 or one may just dance to the big band sounds of the Caribbean Swing Orchestra.

La Boom y Tequila Boom bring you back to the future. Located on Kukulcan Boulevard in the heart of the hotel zone, it's Cancun's primo nightspot. At Tequila Boom, drinks are two for one. It's fun to munch a burger while watching the hot rock 'n roll video, then drift over to La Boom to become a part of the disco's state of the art light and lazer extravaganza.

Ready for the ruins? An evening here should limber you up for the big climb.

View from Presidente Hotel–Isla de Mujeres

Isla de Mujeres
(iss-la day moo-hair-es)

"The crumbling shrine which threatens to topple into the Caribbean is located on the rocky southern coast of the island. Craggy cliffs and a secluded, seaside setting give the place its very special ambience. A visit in the morning–before the tour boats arrive–can be a mystical experience."

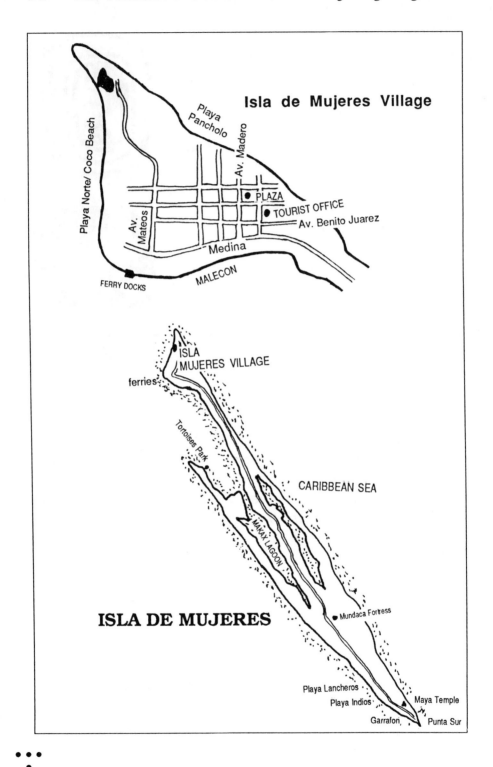

Isla de Mujeres Village

Playa Norte/ Coco Beach

Playa Pancholo

Av. Madero

Av. Mateos

PLAZA

TOURIST OFFICE

Av. Benito Juarez

Medina

MALECON

FERRY DOCKS

ISLA MUJERES VILLAGE

ferries

Tortoises Park

CARIBBEAN SEA

MAKAX LAGOON

ISLA DE MUJERES

Mundaca Fortress

Playa Lancheros

Playa Indios

Maya Temple

Garrafon

Punta Sur

I visited Isla Mujeres for the first time on a "fun" cruise out of Cancun. The attendant hoop-de-doo of other chattering, camera clicking tourists rendered the pilgrimage to the temple of Ixchel a study in frustration. I vowed to return alone and did.

The crumbling shrine which threatens to topple into the Caribbean is located on the rocky southern coast of the island. Craggy cliffs and a secluded, seaside setting give the place its very special ambience. A visit in the morning–before the tour boats arrive–can be a mystical experience.

Half hypnotized by the pounding surf and wild grasses rippling in the wind, I meditated on Ixchel, the Mayan goddess of creativity. Knowing that this place had once been a temple of divination and prayer, I added a silent supplication of my own. "Let the wisdom and spirit of the Maya flow through me–a fusion of intellect and intuition–onto the keys of my typewriter and out into the world."

Did she hear me?

How could I know? . . .The caretakers of the shrine sell shells near the road. There was one peachy pearl spiral that I coveted, but the price was far too high. If the woman lowers her price as I pass by her, I speculated. . . .

She did, *drastically*, and with no attempt at bargaining. I considered it a sign. And still do. The shell sits beside me now.

The Plymouth Rock of Mexico, Isla Mujeres was discovered on March 1, 1517 by Hernandez de Cordoba. The expedition had been beset by misfortunes. Lost and adrift for twenty-one days, the seamen at last sighted the island. What greeted them first were statues of Mayan goddesses standing watch along the coast. Hence the name: Island of Women.

There's another story about how the island got its name. Men seem to prefer it.   Pirates once found the place a convenient retreat in which to hang up their cutlasses and stash their women.   One particularly romantic buccaneer, Antonio de Mundaca, built a luxurious estate, La Hacienda de la Huerta, for his favorite– La Triguena, a beauty with hair the color of wheat.   The remnants of the extensive gardens and the crumbling ruins of the mansion remain to be explored.

Another reminder of a colorful past is Mundaca's tomb, cryptically inscribed: "What I am, you shall be; what you are, I was."

As opposed to Cancun, Isla Mujeres clings tenaciously to its own identity as a fishing village.   People marry, give birth, receive communion, die and are buried here as they have been for centuries.   Fishermen mend their nets and patch their boats seemingly oblivious to the tourists disgorged daily from Cancun..

Slightly raunchy, down at the heels, quite literally going to the dogs–mutts of every description roam free–the tiny island is a beach town plain and simple.

You reach Isla Mujeres by ferry–if driving, from Punta Sam; otherwise from Punta Juarez, both only a few miles north of Cancun.   In either case the price is nominal.   The ferries are wonderful, creaky old vessels where you can sunbath on the deck and dream about handsome pirates or their vast treasures still hidden somewhere on Isla Mujeres.

∴
∴

Ixchel's Temple – Isla de Mujeres

WHERE TO STAY

Once there, it's impossible to miss Isla Mujeres's only *rascacielos* (sky scratcher), **Hotel El Presidente Caribe**. Located in splendid isolation on the northernmost tip of the island, the hotel seems to shimmer like a mirage. It's approached by causeway across a mirror-like lagoon that lends a romantic, other worldly feeling. By Isla Mujeres standards this place is expensive, but would be considered moderate anywhere else. Every one of the 101 rooms is within surf sound of the sea and boasts a magnificent view.

Another pleasant possibility is **Maria's Kin Kan** on the Garrafon Highway. This small, intimate and very romantic beachfront hotel includes an excellent French restaurant.

In the very reasonable range, I've heard raves about the

Hotel Rocamar located near the ferry landing, adjacent to the beach. "Nice people, immaculate accommodations and good food."

WHERE TO EAT

Avenida Hidalgo is lined with restaurants, all much the same. My favorite is *Ciro's* How could you not like a restaurant that serves lobster prepared in a dozen different ways? But don't forget *Maria's Kan Kin* –out on El Garrafon Road, but well worth the walk or short taxi ride.

WHAT TO DO

What to do in Isla Mujeres? We're talking about an island that's only five miles long and in places only one mile wide. You mostly take walks and go to the beach. The ocean extends from white sand in bands of color: first jade, then turquoise, then the blue-green of sub-surface coral reefs and finally the deep marine blue of the open sea.

You can swim through schools of flashing yellow sergeant-majors and parrot fish that flame light gaudy stoplights, but try to get there early before the tourist boats arrive–or most of the fins you see will be made of rubber.

•SHOPPING POSSIBILITES
Shopping in Isla Mujeres is generally unrewarding, very much like Cancun except that the prices are lower. It's best to plan on paying in pesos. Only a few shopkeepers will take traveler's checks or credit cards and the exchange rate on dollars is poor. No one seems to have change here, so paying the exact amount will save you much time and exasperation.

A long midday siesta is observed, stores closing promptly at noon and not opening until four. The most pleasant time to browse is evening.

Casa del Arte Mexicana at Avenue Hidalgo #6 specializes in everything pretty: temple rubbings, batik, black coral, clay reproductions. Close by is ***La Sirena***–very well named. Their windows possess a siren's allure.

•*NIGHT LIFE*

What to do at night? Not much really–unless you count star gazing.

Be prepared with a long wish list, this is the place to get your priorities straight. Later the surf sings love songs, then lullabies.

Presidente Hotel – Isla de Mujeres

Cozumel

Cozumel
(koh-zoo-mell)

"The six mile long Palancar is a massive fortress of coral. Its linear shelf drops steeply from the shallowest level of 10 meters to a depth of 400 meters. This is an ever-changing landscape of towering pinnacles of free standing coral rising as high as 30 meters, arches and tunnels, meandering ravines, blue grottos, dark caves suddenly lit by vivid pink sponges or lacy gorgonia fans. The entire labyrinth is honeycombed with passages leading to sunlit sand flats on the landward side or to a vast electric-blue void on the sea side."

SAN MIGUEL

Av. 5
Av. 10
Av. 15
Av. 20
Av. Rafael Mergar

Calle 4 Norte

Calle 2 Norte

San Miguel Dock

● Palacio Gobireno

● PLAZA

● Tourist Info

Av. Juarez — Road to cross Island ➔

Calle 1 Sur

Calle Rosado Salas

Calle 3 Sur

Car Ferry
to Puerto
Morelos

Hydrofoil Dock

Punta Molas

lighthouse

Cozumel Banks

Isla de la Pasion

San Gervasio ▲

COZUMEL

Cozumel Channel

Hotel Zone

airport

SAN MIGUEL

Caribbean Sea

● Post Office
● Aquarium

Car Ferry

Chancanab Reef

Hotel Zone

Playa Punta Morena

Playa Chen Rio

Chancanab Lagoon & Park

Buena Vista ▲

Playa Punta Chiqueros

Playa San Francisco

El Cedral ▲

Playa de Santa Rosa

Santa Rosa Reef

Playa Palancar

El Caracol ▲
● lighthouse

Palancar Reef

Punta Celerain

Columbria Reef

Maracaibo Reef

C ozumel, which means "Place of Swallows," was sacred from the very beginning. According to the Chilam Balam chronicles ("Books of the Jaguar Soothsayers") this was the Mayan Eden from which the ancients had burst forth "like bees from a hive of honey."

Not surprisingly, the whole island was a kind of shrine to Ixchel, goddess of childbirth, fertility, creativity, the sea and the moon. Since the moon rises in the east and appears to be born out of the sea, it all ties together very well. The moon goddess's effect on the tides was easily observable. When the moon would be full or at its beginning, the tides would soon be at their highest, bountifully spilling fish and crabs onto the beach—a lavish feast waiting to harvested. Obviously Ixchel was a deity to be venerated. Fishermen made sacrifices before Her shrine before setting out to sea and pilgrims from as far away as Belize, Guatemala, Chiapas and Tabasco came to pay homage.

The mysterious moon goddess also possessed the power to prophesy. Sometimes she employed a medium who worked in the same manner as the oracle at Delphi. A high priest inside a large, hollow idol received her messages and transmitted them to the waiting populace. Pilgrimages from the mainland were considered a holy obligation and were particularly popular with pregnant women or women who wished to become pregnant.

Unfortunately it was this Mayan equivalent of Rome or Jerusalem that received the first zealous thrust of Hernan Cortes' idol smashing crusade. In 1519 when the conquistador arrived with his eleven ships and 600 men on their way to conquering all of Mexico, he found an island of some 40,000 inhabitants—twice its present population. Few remnants of Cozumel's former grandeur survived his stay and once the orgy of vandalism was over, the Spaniards lost

interest and abandoned the island to less hypocritical predators.

When the pirates arrived there was nothing left to plunder,
but Cozumel was so desolate that it provided a convenient
hideout similar to Isla Mujeres. Then piracy drifted out of
fashion and the island was abandoned once again.

In 1841 when the famous explorer, John L. Stephens,
arrived with his artist companion, Frederick Catherwood,
Cozumel was a true desert island. "Amid all the
devastations that attended the progress of the Spaniards in
America, none is more complete than that which has swept
over the island of Cozumel," he wrote in his 19th century
travel classic, *Incidents of Travel in Yucatan*. Well, one
form of treasure did remain–and fortunately still does.
Like many contemporary tourists, Stephens was an avid
shell collector. He left the island ladened with Ixchel's
jewels. Who can resist them?

Today one reaches Cozumel easily by plane or ferry boat
navigating between the twin blues of sea and sky. Even
from the air the water is so clear that one can see sandbars
and coral formations.

Once on land the Caribbean influence is more pronounced
than on any other spot in Mexico. Music has a Calypso
beat, food a Creole tang, there's a buccaneer flair to place
names and souvenirs. (Try traveling with a pirate chest–
even a small one–I did. The penalty for temporary insanity
is having to carry home the product of your momentary
madness. Fortunately there *is* life after vacation. The
wooden chest made a dandy Christmas gift filled with
"pieces of eight" candy. The chocolates in their golden foil
are long gone, but my friends still display their brassbound
"treasure" chest.)

It's been estimated that one out of every six visitors to Cozumel comes for the diving. There are shore dives and night dives, refresher courses for intermediates and crash courses for beginners, all taught by experienced bi-lingual dive masters. About one kilometer off the southern end of the island is one of the natural wonders of the undersea world, **Palancar Reef,** second only to Australia's Great Barrier Reef in length.

The six mile long Palancar is a massive fortress of coral. Its linear shelf drops steeply from the shallowest level of 10 meters to a depth of 400 meters. This is an ever-changing landscape of towering pinnacles of free standing coral rising as high as 30 meters, arches and tunnels, meandering ravines, blue grottos, dark caves suddenly lit by vivid pink sponges or lacy gorgonia fans. The entire labyrinth is honeycombed with passages leading to sunlit sand flats on the landward side or to a vast electric-blue void on the sea side.

But Palancar—so heart-stopping in its silent immensity—is only one of many coral subdivisions off Cozumel's southwest coast. Snorkeling, too, is also a visual feast and so, for that matter, is swimming. The whole island is literally surrounded by beach. Taxis are reasonable, but jeeps or mopeds are the best ways to explore the island which is roughly 28 miles long and 11 miles wide. It's exciting to roam the solitary beaches and what's left of the ruins. After an hour passes without seeing another person, you begin to feel like Robinson Crusoe.

Perhaps that's what inspired the popular Robinson Crusoe Cruise. Once there was just one, now there are several from which to choose. Itineraries and destinations vary but all offer a boat trip, seafood picnic and snorkeling.

Part of the entertainment used to be watching the crew catch the fish and lobster that would later become part of the picnic fare. Now most of the area is an aquatic park so the fish course comes out of the sailboat's refrigerator. Too bad in a way, but at least you don't have to worry about eating that charming spindly-legged coral shrimp or the stunning orange and black angel fish you'd encountered while snorkeling.

En route to Palancar Reef

Once during the pre-park days, I noticed one of the other passengers boarding the boat with a pretty conch shell she'd picked up from the scrap pile beside the cooking pot. "I wish I'd gotten one of those," I said aloud as the boat slipped out to sea.

A young crew member heard me and dove overboard. Within seconds he'd returned to the surface holding a much larger shell. His friends pulled him aboard and with a gallant bow he presented it to me.

Well, it was a lovely *thought*, but there I was with a very large shell with a very live conch inside. And here I am still with that very large shell, now on my shelf, minus the original inhabitant.

There's a very unpleasant rumor that the U.S. Army Corps of Engineers delivered the *coup de grace* to Cortes's carnage by plowing under a large Mayan city–until then hidden by dense jungle–during the construction of an airstrip. I try not to think about that when I land at what's now the Cozumel airport.

There are 30 surviving ruins–that we know of. All but two are almost inaccessible. **San Gervasio** is the largest and oldest of those two. Located in Cozumel's northern interior, it's easily reachable by car or moped. Travel eastward on Avenue Juarez (hard-packed limestone roadway) then left on a dirt road (watch for the San Gervasio sign) for about 10 kilometers. You're there.

San Gervasio, dating from the Postclassic Period, is a tumbled mass of raised platforms, crumbled walls and broken columns. Though believed to comprise 120 acres, little has been reclaimed from the jungle. Restrooms and a snack bar have been constructed adjoining the ruins but the most frequent visitors are birds and butterflies. Sometimes the silence is awesome. These monuments to a dead civilization– only a few miles from a very lively one–possess a strange sense of power. The temples and tombs have a magic uniquely their own.

Older yet, probably dating from about 500 A.D., are the ruins at **El Cedral.** They can be easily reached by taking the main highway south out of town past San Francisco Beach. Turn left at the sign and follow a paved road just over 3 kilometers. Surprisingly, this small ruin with a tree sprouting from its roof still bears a few traces of the original paint. The place is a study in contrast. The exposed roots of the living tree hold the ancient stones in a strange embrace and nearby there's a tiny church where one can see among the artifacts evidence of the continuing compromise between Christianity and native religion.

The Mayas have endowed the saints with very human attributes. These beings are not unfailingly benevolent. Rather they're neutral like the ancient gods, and can be just as capricious. Not only is deference to their status demanded, but attention to their physical comfort. Garments must be frequently washed and worn ones replaced. Offerings of chocolate and tortillas may often be found before the Virgin and other saintly favorites.

WHERE TO STAY ─────────────────────

Cozumel has only one town, San Miguel. Hotels here are convenient and inexpensive. A perennial favorite because of the very low tariff is **Hotel Yoly.** ("Holy Yoly") Upscale but still moderate for Cozumel is the **Hotel Vista del Mar.** Most rooms have a sea view and a tiny balcony facing out on the public beach.

My sentimental favorite in the first class beach front category is the well preserved old timer, **Hotel Cozumel Caribe.** Well located on the classically tropical coconut-palm-studded San Juan Beach, it offers, in addition to your basic paradise ambience, a wide variety of water sports.

Another attractive alternative is **La Ceiba Beach Hotel** at Paradise Point on the southern coast. Here, boat trips to

Palancar Reef, night dives and lessons, etc., are also stressed. As an added attraction, there's the opportunity to explore a War II plane deliberately sunk about 50 yards offshore during the filming of the movie *Cyclone*.

WHERE TO EAT

Three favorites as different as restaurants can be, but all very, very good:

•*Morgan's* (named, of course, for Henry, the pirate, who used to hang out around Cozumel) on the main plaza offers the freshest lobster and the coldest margaritas in town. The bananas flambe are a specialty that definitely lives up to the spectacular promise.

•*Pizza Rolandion*–crazy as it sounds to eat pizza in Mexico, this is a class act operation by any standards any place. The courtyard with its giant shade trees and lush tropical plants is charming.   The Four Seasons Pizza is excellent and inexpensive, but so are the other Italian specialties: Serrano ham, cannelloni, lasagna.

•*Restaurant Las Palmeras* just a few doors down near the zocolo is the "real thing," an authentic Mexican restaurant. Breakfast, lunch and dinner are all served here with traditional Mexican favorites, plus guava con queasy (guava paste with cheese and crackers)–a pleasant and unexpected touch of the Mexican gourmet.

WHAT TO DO

•SHOPPING

The only art form unique to Quintana Roo is handworked jewelry made from black coral. This comes primarily from the reefs around Cozumel. You'll find coral jewelry everywhere. *Mercado de Artesanias* (craft market) , just behind the plaza, is a good place to begin your search; but *Van Cleef,* immediately north of the craft market, has the most stunning collection.

Isn't it nice to know that—besides being beautiful—black coral is literally good for what ails you? Traditionally it's been known to possess healing power and the ability to ward off evil.

Black coral is made up of thousands of tiny jelly-like animals encased in calcium carbonate shells. These small animals, called polyps, group together in colonies in shapes similar to sea fans and thrive on the microscopic plants and animals carried in the ocean currents.

Black coral is rare because it grows only in a few areas of the world in water temperatures of 50 degrees Fahrenheit or warmer. The water must also be free of sediment, sand and mud. What better place than the crystalline waters of the Mexican Caribbean? Here, divers using regular scuba equipment descend to depths of 70 meters in search of black coral colonies. The coral used to be found much nearer the water's surface, but because of uncontrolled exploitation, divers must continually look deeper. Once a colony is located, it's removed by divers with a saw, hammer or chisel. When exposed to the air, black coral becomes very hard, allowing it to be worked into beads and drilled.

Divers from Cozumel have the monopoly on black coral

because of their hard won expertise and their accessibility to the reefs. It's also primarily artisans from that island who transform the coral into necklaces, pendants, bracelets and earrings. Each black coral colony is carefully studied to decide from which part the beads will be made or from which area the fragile twigs will be taken. Next comes the tedious job of polishing and shaping each piece with the help of a machine similar to a dentist's drill. Some pieces are smoothed into round or irregular shaped beads. Other pieces, stems and twigs, are left unmodified except for polishing. The fragments are then drilled and strung into jewelry.

Whether worn to ward of an evil eye or attract a roving one, the effect is sheer black magic.

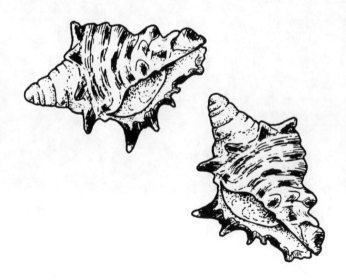

Aventuras Akumel

The Mexican Caribbean

"Distances cease to exist as strangely contorted trees, towering plants of emerald green, feathery ferns, spongy fungus all crowd close together. When you can drive no farther, a narrow path snakes its way through the lush foliage dotted by brilliant azure morning glories. Vines writhe their way up through the damp, dark soil. Most look strong enough to support Tarzan."

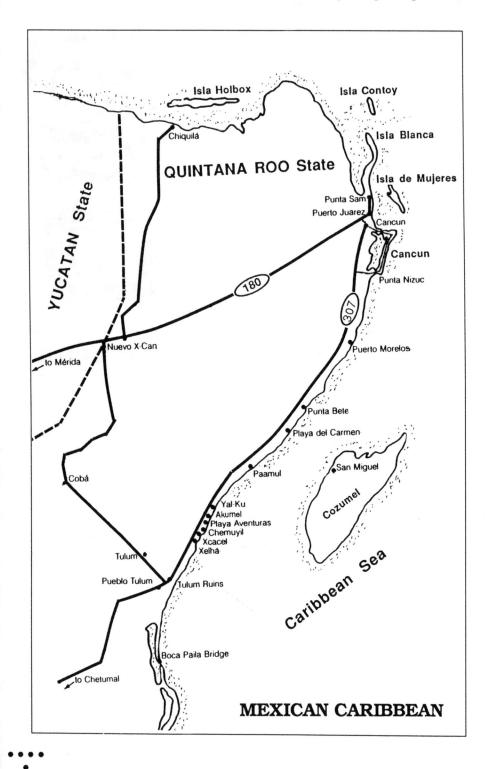

Isla Holbox

Isla Contoy

Chiquilá

Isla Blanca

QUINTANA ROO State

Isla de Mujeres

YUCATAN State

Punta Sam
Puerto Juarez
Cancun

Cancun

180

Punta Nizuc

307

Nuevo X·Can

to Mérida

Puerto Morelos

Punta Bete

Playa del Carmen

Cobá

Paamul

San Miguel

Yal·Ku
Akumel
Playa Aventuras
Chemuyil
Xcacel
Xelhá

Cozumel

Tulum

Caribbean Sea

Pueblo Tulum

Tulum Ruins

Boca Paila Bridge

to Chetumal

MEXICAN CARIBBEAN

"There was nothing standing;
Only the clam water, the placid sea, alone and tranquil.
Nothing existed.

"Then they planned the creation,
And the growth of the trees and the tickets and the birth of life.

"Thus let it be done!
Let the emptiness be filled!
Let the water recede and make a void.
Let the earth appear and become solid;
Let it be done, thus they spoke.
Let there be light, let there be dawn in the sky and the earth!
                              Popol Vuh

W hen the gods concluded their divine dialogue, the jungle was born. It exists now virtually as it did then—a forest primeval. And at its edge laps the eternal sea.

Heading south from Cancun on Highway 307 the road is well paved and arrow straight. On either side is dense, green jungle, enticing to some, vaguely disturbing to others. Who knows what silent, slinking predators watch, listen, wonder at the humans roaring by seemingly oblivious to them.

A stop at Xcaret (sha-ret) is a time trip to a pre-historic era. A wooden sign on the left hand side of the road marks the way but a better landmark is the restaurant literally covered with flaming hibiscus blossoms. (A good place to eat: excellent fish soup and fried bananas, a nice owner, pleasant music kept to a low roar.) Bearing off to the left down the dirt road one sees thatched cottages and turkeys, many, many turkeys.

Soon the jungle begins again closing in on either side of the narrow road. Distances cease to exist as strangely contorted trees, towering plants of emerald green, feathery ferns, spongy fungus all crowd close together. When you can drive no farther, a narrow path snakes its way through the lush foliage dotted by brilliant azure morning glories. Vines writhe their way up through the damp, dark soil. Most look strong enough to support Tarzan.

Soon you begin to see the Mayan ruins and possibly the archeologists who've begun the Humpty Dumpty task of repositioning the stones that have tumbled into rubble. Since most of the buildings contain altars, this is believed to have been a ceremonial site.

At the end of the path is a tiny bay so clear that the brightly colored fish sparkle in the sunlight, but the best treat is to be experienced on the return. Turn right at the ruins and follow the trail to a cave entrance leading to a hidden cenote or pool–incredibly cool and blue. Small wonder the ancients considered them to be sacred–as do some of the moderns.

I'd just lowered myself into the water, savoring the cool remoteness when the vines at the entrance to the cavern parted. A man clambered toward me over the rocks, both arms a-jingle with silver bracelets he'd come to sell. Trouble in paradise? Well, at least a two-legged tempter.

——— AN UNEXPECTED SURPRISE ———

The room darkened suddenly, mysteriously. Behind the white-draped altar the high priest officiated. Beside him two silent neophytes watched every move. I recognized this man instantly; I'd seen his face depicted many times on tombs and temples. I knew the proud, haughty nose, the grim, unsmiling mouth.

His hands moved deftly, the dark eyes gleaming triumphantly as flames shot higher and higher, a burst of brilliant blue casting eerie shadows in a room gone silent.

The expression on the dark face changed into a charming smile as, with a flourish, he leaned forward and presented me with a plate of crepe suzettes.

The rite was symbolic of *Aventuras Akumel,* an enclave of elegance literally carved out of jungle. This place is so unique, so totally terrific that a part of me hates to write about it. Aventuras Akumel is too good to last. One needn't possess the Mayan gift of prophecy to know that. You can hear its death knell every time a fume-spewing tour bus roars by on its way to Tulum.

The "high priest"speaks no English or Spanish, only Mayan. He comes from a village of fifty—forty-nine since his recent defection—deep in the hinterlands. It seems incredible that a man growing up without electricity could rise so rapidly to master chef. Perhaps that's why he's so good at flaming dishes. Besides crepe suzettes, brandied sauces, Mexican coffee, and bananas flambe are menu highlights. He does a fantastic caesar salad as well (and this is one of those rare places in Mexico where it's safe to eat it.)

Almost over night a transformation is taking place. You can hear the Mayan staff each morning at their English class. ("Hell-oh," "Good Mor-ning," "R yoo fin-ished?") Condominiums are under construction. You can monitor their progress as workmen pass by carrying beams, couches and toilet tanks.

The hotel rooms would be a visual feast anywhere, their whimsy and sophistication a double delight in the midst of a wilderness. On one side a balcony looks out over waving palms and a tiny boat landing. Yes, it *is* possible. Beaches really can be that dazzling white, water can be the color of jade—the jade of a priceless Chinese pendant.

But on the other side is a jungle that seems to stretch on forever, seemingly impenetrable, teeming with life: parrots, spider monkeys, alligators, jaguars.

Legends abound in the jungle, tales of sacred animals, magical plants; just as the seas bear testimony to the daring of Jean Lafitte, Black Beard and Anne Bonney who slashed and swaggered their way into the already colorful pages of Mayan history.

The pirate legacy is very much a part of the ambience of Aventuras Akumel. The hotel complex is headquarters for Cedam, an organization of underwater archeologists. The divers "discovered" Akumel in 1958 while exploring the wreck of the Spanish galleon *El Matanzero*. Soon they also came upon submerged Mayan ruins where the sea had engulfed the land. The place became—and still is—an "in" spot for divers who fly there in private planes. Now the grounds and buildings are filled with remnants of ancient sailing ships; and the new hotel has its own muscum

Outdoor cenote – next to Xel-ha

sailing ships; and the new hotel has its own museum which includes pewter tankards and swords retrieved from the deep as well as Pre-Columbian artifacts found in the jungle.

Tomorrow Aventuras Akumel may be another Cancun. Today it's paradise.

To the south of Aventuras Akumel on the left side of the road is **Xel-ha** (shell-ha), probably the largest   natural

Xel-ha

aquarium in the world. It's also the busiest around tour bus time. If you can possibly time your arrival to be in **Xel-ha** when the buses are in Tulum, your enjoyment will be increased immeasurably. But at any hour, this place is not to be missed.

Xel-ha is a true swimmer's paradise for there's no undertow. A vast labyrinth of underwater caves and tunnels, it covers approximately ten square acres. There are some fifty or so species of fish in every imaginable hue crying out to be admired.

Even if you're not a swimmer, you need only slip into the cool, crystal water and wait for the fish to come to you. It's an incredible experience to feel them. Should you tire of fish and fish stories, lie on the wharf and listen to the gentle lapping of the water as you read a good old fashioned bodice ripper. (Will the planter's daughter be ravished by the pirate crew or will their handsome captain reserve her for himself?) You'll have to bring your own novel. Snorkeling equipment can be rented on the spot.

Only a short distance south of the lagoon on the right hand side of the road are the Mayan ruins of Xel-ha. Though these begin only a few feet from the highway, passersby rarely see them—a sad omission. Like Xaret, the lush jungle setting is magical. The ruins are extensive and well preserved, the wall paintings even clearer than the ones at Tulum.

If you're fortunate, the sometime caretaker may come around and show you the way to the cenote. Write your own script, live your own movie, this is the place. We're talking spectacular! The most beautiful outdoor cenote on the Yucatan Peninsula.

WHERE TO STAY & EAT ───────────────

Calypso Club Lafitte Caribe on the Cancun-Tulum road at Punta Bete has a charming ambience. Attractive bungalows with baths and private terraces face the sea. The bar-restaurant is lively, the staff eager, friendly, helpful. "Our knowledge of the ocean is our strength," is the motto. The emphasis is on diving with a staff of professionals, and a more than ample supply of tanks and boats available. Prices are moderate.

At *Motel El Crucero,* they're *cheap* . The atmosphere here is zero, but the accommodations are clean, adequate and very convenient to the Tulum ruins. El Crucero is located at the junction of Highway 307 and the Tulum access road. Anyone traveling by bus or on a tight budget couldn't do better. There's an adequate, equally inexpensive restaurant with an even better one—*Restaurant El Paisan y El Venado*— just across the street.

The *Cabanas Chac-Mool* are located three miles south of the Tulum ruins. It would be difficult to exaggerate the beauty of the location, the price is super low, the food excellent. I had lobster every night. I also had bedbugs. The thatched hut is a real palapa furnished with a chair, a table and two beds suspended on ropes from the ceiling.

When the swinging motion made one guest seasick, he removed the mattress and placed it on the the floor. The next day the staff had elevated it once again. "*Animales!,*" they warned him. What kind of *animales?* I wondered. Rats? Scorpions? Fortunately I saw neither, though I did have some surprising encounters in the communal uni-sex bathroom.

Accommodations, like everything else, come down to a matter of choices.

El Castillo–Tulum from the northside

Tulum
(too-loom)

"Mounted on the edge of a cliff, this abandoned city towers above one of the most uniquely beautiful beaches in the world. Yes, it is possible to dodge the crowd, find a quiet corner and meditate on the mysteries of the Mayan world—or one's own world."

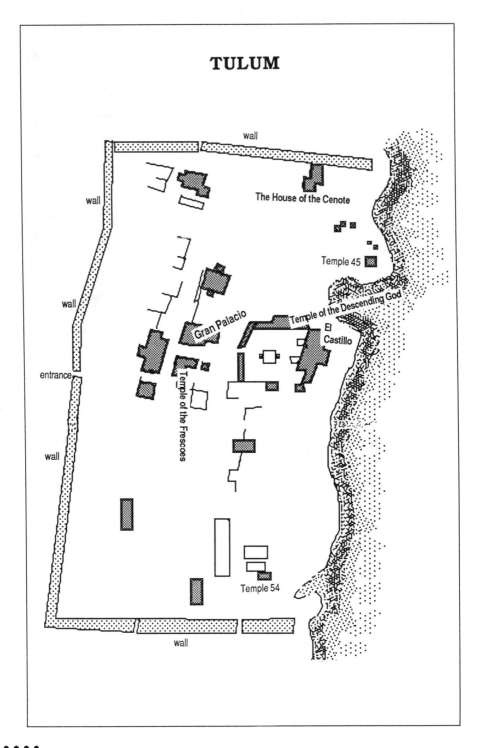

TULUM

wall

wall

wall

The House of the Cenote

Temple 45

entrance

Gran Palacio

Temple of the Descending God

El Castillo

Temple of the Frescoes

wall

Temple 54

wall

Five kilometers south of Akumal on Hwy. 307, a side road leads to Tulum. Here early morning light awakens the "City of the Dawn." A mariner's landmark perched high above the opalescent waters of the Caribbean, the fortress city watched over traders gliding by on large dugout canoes ladened with jade, feathers, honey, and the precious cacao beans used for money. Mounted on the summit of a limestone cliff 40 feet high, lashed by waves of open sea, the high, thick fortification walls bespeak local feuds. One of the last strongholds of a dying civilization, Tulum was sighted by the Spaniards in 1517, within 50 years the city lay silent.

Everybody who was anybody lived *in* Tulum. This city which reached its apogee between 1000 A.D. and 1600 A.D., during the decline of the Mayan civilization, was set aside for nobles and highly esteemed merchants or warriors. Except for slaves serving their masters, the lower classes were kept out.

That rigid selectivity is believed to have been the undoing of the place. Ultimately the peasants who lived outside the walled city revolted. All that remains today of the proud citadel are ruins.

Though the beginnings of Tulum stretch back into earliest time, the majority of its structures are from the Postclassic or "decadent" period. For this reason, Tulum often gets short shrift from classic scholars who tend to write it off as "bourgeois" or even "miserable." This attitude ignores the strength of the architecture—said to have inspired Frank Lloyd Wright himself—and the organizational skill of the people who built these massive structures.

It also overlooks the esthetic and prophetic significance of the seaside setting. Originally called Zama, or "place of the dawning," this was the most important of the strategically located ceremonial centers. It was from the seas beyond the walls that the sun rose each morning and began her sacred dance across the skies, and it was from that same sea that the Spaniards first appeared.

In 1511 a Spanish ship was wrecked off the coast of Jamaica. The survivors drifted ashore at what was by then called Tulum, or walled city, in a small boat. What they saw was a showplace. Every stone was covered with brilliant paintings and carvings–stark white, deep red or vibrant blue backgrounds covered with multi-colored stylized figures. At the top of the largest building–the castillo or castle, as they called it–a beacon fire blazed.

Five of the men including their captain were killed by the wary Mayas well aware of an ancient prophecy that warned of bearded men who would come out of the sea to rob them of their land. The two remaining survivors, Gonzalo Guerrero and Jeronimo de Aguilar, had to talk fast to save their lives. Somehow they were able to convince their captors that they were strong and resourceful, an asset to the community.

Aguilar was eventually sold as a slave to a passing trader and taken to Cozumel where he remained until freed by Cortés's invasion. Guerrero went native. Before long he was speaking fluent Mayan and moving freely, so freely that he became a military leader and married the daughter of a king.

In 1517 another Spaniard, Juan de Grijalva, sailed by and was so impressed by the sea view of Tulum that he literally wrote home about it: "We sailed a day and a night, and on the following day at sunset, we descried a citadel, or a city, so large that Seville seemed to us neither larger nor better."

Before long a Spanish expedition was sent to pacify and conquer the "islands" of Cozumel and Yucatan. It was Guerrero who incited the Mayas to fight fate. *He* hadn't heard the prophecy and refused to give credence to it. Francisco Herandez de Cordoba was merely a man like himself and could be defeated. Guerrero's battle strategies depended upon surprise attacks, ambushes and cunning. The modern day term guerrilla warfare gets its name from the tactics he introduced.

When the Spaniards were repulsed in Tulum, Cortés offered Guerrero amnesty, sending his old comrade Aguilar with gifts and a promise that the prodigal son would be well received. Guerrero's reply has never been forgotten:
"Brother Aguilar, I am a married man, I have three children. They (the Mayas) hold me as a chief and a captain during wars. Go with God, for my face is carved and my ears pierced. What would the Spaniards say about me, when they see me in this manner! You have seen my children, how lovely they are. For your life, if for them you'd give me these green beads which you have brought I shall say that my brothers have sent me from my land."

The three children of Guerrero and his Mayan princess are the first recorded mestizos, the first known blending of Indian and Spanish blood.

The fall of Tulum occurred about fifty years after the Spanish invasion of the Yucatan Peninsula but was unrelated to it. The Mayas–both triumphant peasants and defeated overlords–left the area. For a time pirates took advantage of the little cove below El Castillo; but by 1842 when John Stephens and Frederick Catherwood arrived, the place was deserted.

The terrain was so desolate that it reminded Stephens "of

the witches' gathering place in the Hartz Mountains, as described in Faust of Goethe." Later, "an image of a grove sacred to Druidical worship" came to him as he climbed the once grand staircase of **El Castillo** then overgrown with thick green foliage and looked about at the mysterious buildings that surrounded him.

I experienced some of Stephens' sensations in 1966 when I stepped out of a small plane chartered in Cozumel and surveyed Tulum for the first time.   Much of the site was obscured by jungle. The steps, the platform and the vast area before **El Castillo** were overgrown by trees. Great vines seemed to writhe up out of the ground twining their way about the columns.

Years passed, my next trip was by tour bus.   When I stepped off the air conditioned vehicle, I discovered that the pirates had returned.   They waved and beckoned from small shops pointing out a colorful assortment of blankets, crafts, and jewelry at double the price of the nearby villages. Once inside the gate I found that the whole site had been cleared. Tulum now looks like a golf course.

Well, so much the better to see, but still a part of me envies Stephens when he wrote:

"We had undertaken our long journey to this place in utter uncertainty as to what we should meet with; impediments and difficulties had accumulated upon us, but already we felt indemnified for all our labor. We were amid the wildest scenery we had yet found in Yucatan; and, besides the deep and exciting interest in the ruins themselves, we had around us what we wanted in all the other places, the magnificence of nature. Clearing away the platform in front, we looked over an immense forest; walking around the molding of the wall, we looked out upon the boundless ocean, and deep in the clear water at the foot of the cliff we saw gliding quietly a great fish eight or ten feet long."

View of Tulum's famous El Castillo

The party camped in **El Castillo** and one night when a tropic storm came up Stephens wrote of "the darkness, the howling of the winds, the cracking of branches in the forest, the dashing of angry waves against the cliff. . ." But on another night "the moon was shining magnificently, lighting up the darkness of the forest, and drawing a long silvery line upon the sea. . . " They felt themselves "exalted above the necessity of sleep." Instead he philosophized, "The city no longer keeps watch; the fiat of destruction has gone out against it, and in solitude it rests, the abode of silence and desolation."

There is very little silence or solitude to be had in Tulum at tour time, but the setting is still stunning. Mounted on the edge of a cliff, this abandoned city towers above one of the most uniquely beautiful beaches in the world. Yes, it is possible to dodge the crowd, find a quiet corner and meditate on the mysteries of the Mayan world—or one's own world.

The city is still effectively enclosed. A veritable barbed wire fence of cactus and other thorny plants covers the cliffs. On the other three sides Tulum is protected by a great wall 3,600 feet in length and averaging 15 to 20 feet in height broken only by five narrow gateways admitting but one person at a time. Beyond the guardhouses stationed at the western end, a solid mass of vegetation extends into the alligator-infested swamps that stretch for miles inland.

The present day Mayas say that in ancient times Tulum was connected to Coba, Chichen Itza and Uxmal by means of a skyroad called a *cuxan san* (living rope). One can only wonder about where this enigmatic fragment fits into the

Jungle encroaches on Tulum

giant Mayan puzzle. What we do know is that *sacbes* or stone causeways connected all the ceremonial centers so that traders and supplicants alike could pass easily through the jungle. Tulum's northeast gate was the sallyport to the *sacbe* that lead to Xelha, six miles away, and that some place close by was a turnoff point westward to Coba and on to Chichen Itza.

Most of the buildings of Tulum share a unique architectural characteristic. The walls are slightly flared upward. This inverted pyramid effect creates areas of light and shadow that not only enhance the sculptured relief but also protect the painted stucco moldings from rain water.

The most dominant building in Tulum was called **El Castillo** by the Spaniards because if it looked like a castle, it must be one. Who knows, perhaps they were right.

Besides its spectacular view of the sea, **El Castillo** has a mystery to ponder–the red hand prints on its inner wall. Are they the imprint of a living hand? Thinking so brings me closer to the builders of the city. I like to imagine that across the time, the desolation, the stillness and the mystery–another human being reaches out to greet me.

This great temple is made up of three terraced stories, each of which bears a small sanctuary. Its monumental effect is accented by a broad central stairway that rises to the top terrace and leads to the main sanctuary.

Flanking **El Castillo** are two smaller structures, prosaically designated by archaeologists as **Temples 45** and **54. Temple 54** is close to the sea and the southern wall. Despite the remoteness of the area and its apparent desolation, Stephens believed this temple was still in use. To the north of **El Castillo** is **Temple 45** which is actually the largest of several offertories. It was here that prayers were offered to Ixchel. Today one can look out as the ancients must have done at the pretty cove below and 400 yards beyond to a "blue hole,"–the sea's equivalent of a cenote.
The only really ugly cenote that I've come across thus far is

● ● ●

located close by. Adjacent to the eastern gate of the north wall is the **House of the Cenote**. Where there are cenotes, there are invariably nearby temples where offerings were made and gods propitiated by sacrifices and ritual bathing. Here the temple sits above the roof of the cave. It appears to have been built in two different stages. The original building had two chambers with an entrance facing the sea and an altar in the inner room. Later a smaller room was added on the southeastern corner with steps leading into the cave and additional steps running around the mouth of the cenote and down to the bottom of the cavern which is almost at sea level. Unfortunately the cave is full of bats which have an unfortunate effect on the water. It takes a great deal of imagination to visualize what was once a prime source of physical and spiritual well-being.

The **Temple of the Frescoes** is located directly in front of **El Castillo** on "Main Street." This temple has been added on to many times. The Mayas believed that the world came to an end every 52 years (theirs was a 52-year calendar cycle.) The ending was celebrated by canceling debts, the beginning or rebirth by building higher and more elegant structures over the base of older ones. One can easily see the effects of this custom here. First there was a small square single room with a door facing the street, a curved roof rising almost from the floor and an altar on the rear wall. This is now the inner temple of the first floor. The remains of the rich wall murals were preserved by the additions.

A later gallery was added along three sides with four columns on the street side and two on the north and south ends. The walls are covered with greenish blue paintings against a black background. Two of the biggies in the godly pantheon, Ixchel and Chac, are portrayed here along with sacred serpents and more red handprints. These 13th

• • • •

century wall paintings are quite beautiful, but require a flashlight to see to best advantage. The most recent addition is a small upper deck with a single door facing Main Street. There's a small altar here against the rear wall and a curved vaulted roof.

The most intriguing and controversial of all the buildings in Tulum is the **Temple of the Descending God** located to the immediate left of **El Castillo**. The base of the building is an older structure that's been filled in to support the newer one. A stairway emerges into a single chamber with a window on the sea. One either side are two ceremonial benches. The blue mural represents the night sky with Venus–sacred to the Mayas–and other stars combined with mythic serpents. In the center are numerous deities from the Mayan pantheon which is as vast as the stars themselves.

But it's the figure above the temple doorway that's most impressive. This is a large carved figure of a deity descending head first. The conventional theory is that the carving depicts Ab Muzen Cab, the Mayan bee god. (In Pre Columbian times, as today, honey was a mainstay of the Yucatean diet.) A more provocative one suggests that the descending god is an extra terrestrial. Could he be in some way connected to the *cuxan san* or the skyway legend?

Coba's history is written here

Coba
(koh-bah)

"The canopy of foliage overhead is like a green cloud cover over the jungle floor. Toucans, macaws, and turquoise-crested motmots are a brilliant burst of color against the sacred ceiba trees hung with Spanish moss. Even at midday it's a green twilight zone—every growing thing, even the petals of flowers seem to exude a warm, moist stickiness that's dense and thick to breathe like some kind of clear fog. Not too far away monkeys screech, deer and jaguar slip in and out of forest shadows. The jungle smells spicy, musky, ripe and sweet—the odors of rampant growth rooted in old decay."

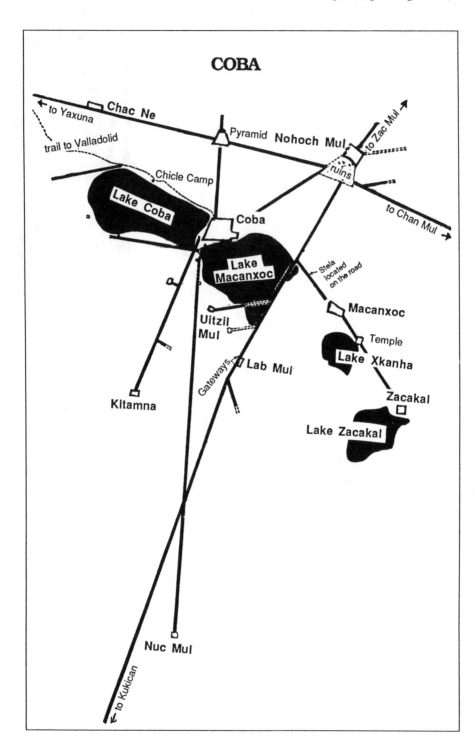

COBA

I   t was in Coba (koh-bah) that I first learned the true meaning of the expression, "One step at a time." **Nohoch Mul Pyramid** has 120 steps and is thought to be the tallest in Mexico. It's a steep climb, the steps narrow and uneven; but once at the top, the view is breathtaking. Of course, what goes up must come down. That was even worse–until I caught onto the jaguar crawl. Think about it.

Walking about Coba would be exciting even without the ruins. The canopy of foliage overhead is like a green cloud cover over the jungle floor. Toucans, macaws, and turquoise-crested motmots are a brilliant burst of color against the sacred ceiba trees hung with Spanish moss. Even at midday it's a green twilight zone–every growing thing, even the petals of flowers seem to exude a warm, moist stickiness that's dense and thick to breathe like some kind of clear fog. Not too far away monkeys screech, deer and jaguar slip in and out of forest shadows. The jungle smells spicy, musky, ripe and sweet–the odors of rampant growth rooted in old decay.

But the ruins do exist–80 square miles of them. This was one of the largest cities on the Yucatan Peninsula with a population of 500,000. Where are they now, one wonders, looking at the remains of this tumble-down, jungle-covered city spread along the shores of five blue lakes.

As I rested at the top of **Nohoch Mul**, I watched a man slowly toiling his way up. Too macho for the jaguar crawl, he was having a hard time of it. Going down would prove even worse despite his gallant efforts to appear casual.) Once at the top, he turned panting to survey the scene below. "Wow! It's a jungle out there!" he gasped.

We laughed at the cliche come so literally to life. Below us

••••

was a shag rug of rich emerald dotted by five blobs of turquoise–the lakes which once endowed the city with its water
supply.   Here and there large rocky mounds overgrown
with foliage offer the exciting potential of fresh discovery.
There are few tourists and one can sit quietly contemplating
these treasures in solitude.

Coba was a "lost" city until the late 1920s when J. Eric
Thompson did some preliminary exploration, but excavations didn't begin until 1973.   Very little has been reconstructed or even uncovered of the estimated 6500 structures
on the site.

The city is designated as Classic, dating from around 600 to
900 A.D., but there are Preclassic indications on some of
the buildings and definite Postclassic additions to the original Classic motifs. The Spaniards never found Coba but for
some reason the inhabitants abandoned it. Today the few
remaining Mayan descendants live resignedly in grass
shacks on the outskirts of this vast ghost city. Where did
their ancestors go?   Why did they go? How did they support
themselves in a land where almost nothing grows today?
What happened to their vast culture?

So many missing pieces to the Mayan puzzle.

One of the features that distinguishes Coba is the prominence of a female figure which frequently appears on the facades of its buildings. Many archaeologists believe that she
was a ruler involved in a ritualistic marriage with a high
priest from Tikal. This would explain why the ruins are so
similar to those found in the Peten region of Guatemala and
so unlike anything in Yucatan. Coba will probably prove to
be the largest archaeological site in Mexico. **Nohoch Mul
Pyramid** alone is built on the grand scale of the Peten pyramids, rising a full twelve stories above the jungle.

Coba is the hub of a complex network of causeways called *sacbes* that fanned out in at least fifty directions to other Mayan cities on the Peninsula. The longest of these stretches for 62.3 miles through dense jungle with no curves all the way to Chichen Itza. One of them even crosses the arm of one of the lakes. The roads, which were constructed with tollgates, were used as trade and messenger arterials as well ceremonial routes. There were no dray animals or wheels used, so the Mayas carried everything on their backs – including their chieftains who were born on litters.

One of Coba's beautiful lakes

Legend has it that King Ucan unrolled the roads or causeways like a ribbon from a stone on his shoulders. All went smoothly until a beautiful woman appeared to tempt him. When she beckoned seductively, the chaste, work-a-holic monarch averted his gaze. Though he tried to avoid her, she blocked his way. Eventually he dropped his stone and reached for her. Suddenly his magic powers vanished.

King Ucan's inability to lift the stone abruptly ended the construction project.

Today the efforts of King Ucan — or somebody — are almost entirely obscured by jungle. These level roads made of local limestone over a rock base are engineering masterpieces, yet a single seed falling into a declivity in the limestone can take root in the jungle atmosphere. Barely discernible, the sacbes remain a marvel.

A few yards from the entrance to the site is the **Grupo Coba** dominated by the 105-step pyramid called the **"Church."** To the right are several tall structures surrounding a court. One contains an inner chamber with a Korbel arch roof. The Korbel arch with its gracefully upward tapering shape appears

Illustrations of various Korbel arches

again and again in Mayan architecture and is considered a unique engineering achievement. Old world structures of the same era were built with a keystone and would have collapsed without it. The Mayas had no need for a keystone.

Off to the right of the main road is **Las Pinturas Group.** The main pyramid here is an easier climb. From the temple at the top one can look through the window and see **Nohuch Mul** framed as though in a picture. The frescoes are still plainly visible, lovely muted shades of red and turquoise.

About a mile further is **Conjunto Macanxoc** where the finest *stelae* —yet discovered—are found. Here as in other *stelae* (stone slabs generally set in front of prominent structures containing information about the building and/ or important people of the era) throughout the site, the theme appears to be that of dominance. One figure, presumably a subject or captive, kneels before an overlord. These *stelae* are truly magnificent, one rising as high as ten feet. Local tradition has it that a group of people referred to as the *pus'ob* , or dwarfs, were responsible for the *stelae* that dot the inner core of the city. The *pus'ob* are said to have drowned in a self-inflicted deluge that brought an end to the fourth creation of the Maya world.

The most distant and dramatic of the excavated pyramids is the previously mentioned **Nohuch Mul.** Once you've caught your breath at the top, you'll note three niches over the door of the temple containing descending gods similar to those at Tulum. Bee gods or space cadets? A question to ponder as you look out over the vast expanse of jungle below. The view is particularly spectacular at sunrise or sunset when the shadows accent the myriad mounds of yet unexplored pyramids below.

All along the main trail beguiling paths lure one to new adventures. It's easy to imagine the appeal of archaeology. It's also easy to get lost or at least distracted. There's so much to cover. One could spend a long time at Coba and not see it all.

On the trail one hears almost as many French and German accents as American and Texan. As the smartly dressed Frenchwomen pass (yes, even here they manage to achieve a kind of bush chic), the scent you catch is more apt to be insect repellent than Yves St. Laurent. The "moschetoes" as Stephens called them are very prevalent.

> Coba is a quick, easy drive by car. Proceed south past the Tulum Ruins Junction for 2 kilometers, then turn west on the clearly marked Coba Highway. Coba is 45 kilometers or 26 miles from the main highway. Coba is also reachable by bus from Cancun or Merida, but schedules vary and should be checked and then rechecked.

WHERE TO STAY & WHERE TO EAT

"Accommodations in Coba go from paradise to the pits," a travel agent once told me.

What I subsequently learned from this is that paradise is a very relative thing. The Villa Arqueologica Coba isn't my idea of it. Still it's pleasant to find a clean, imaginatively furnished hotel overlooking a placid lake in the midst of a jungle. Rooms are a series of white plastered niches and arches neatly furnished, bathrooms are clean. Common rooms are enhanced by excellent reproductions of Mayan sculpture and blow ups of old Pancho Villa photographs.

Considering that the place is run by the Club Med, I expected more than I got. The drinks were weak and vastly overpriced. The menu listings make the mouth water but failed to live up to their promise. Guests grumbled. There was talk of taking up a collection to send the chef to Paris for additional training. The next evening I discovered that it would only be necessary to send him half a block away.

El Bocadito, also adjacent to the lake, has delicious food practically for pennies. Five of us ordered five different specialties and shared. It was all extremely good. El Bocadito also has a few rooms for rent. I wouldn't describe them as the pits, but they are spartan—they're also much in demand. If this is your style, get there early as there's no phone.

Nohoch Mul Pyramid

Lobby of Hotel El Meson del Marquez

Valladolid
(vie-a-do-lit)

"Nowhere in the Americas is there more of a sense of duality than in Mexico. The extremes of night and day, birth and death, plenty and poverty, light and shadow are interwoven into every aspect of the culture."

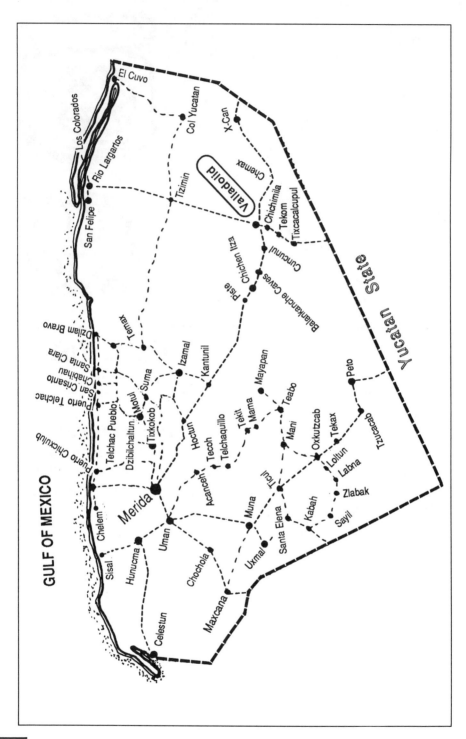

N owhere in the Americas is there more of a sense of duality than in Mexico. The extremes of night and day, birth and death, plenty and poverty, light and shadow are interwoven into every aspect of the culture.

In ancient times both priest and peasant were painfully aware of the moon goddess's effect upon the tides. Ixchel could bring not only fertility and abundance but destruction. From the deep wells of the subconscious came gifts of prophecy and creativity but also dark visions of disaster. With her headdress of twined serpents and jaguar claw fingernails, Ixchel could be the stuff of nightmares.

Twin images of birth and death are equally prevalent today. The tree of life is a perennially popular motif, but so is the skull. Children play with dolls in the likeness of skeletons; confectioners make little skulls of sugar.

Valladolid is a striking manifestation of such duality, its turbulent history rooted in birth, death and inevitable transformation. Today Valladolid is a terrific town with a terrible past. Originally a ceremonial center named for Zaci, its sacred cenote, the name was pre-emptively changed by the conquistadors to honor Valladolid, the Spanish city where Ferdinand and Isabella were married.

Here the Mayas fought valiantly to protect their ritual citadel and reprisals against them were particularly brutal. Leading families were forced into their homes and burned alive. Women were hanged with their children suspended from their feet. In one object lesson a virgin and a young bride were slaughtered by a Spanish commander. They were selected simply because they were beautiful. The act was a mixed message. The officer sought to remove temptation from his troops while demonstrating to the Mayas that his men weren't interested in their women.

The Mayas possess long memories. In 1848 they managed to raise an army of their own and launched the "War of the Castes." The hierarchy of Valladolid was comprised of direct descendants of the Spanish conquerors intensely proud of their heritage. That elitist attitude cost them dearly. Vengeance was savage. Daughters of the grandees were raped, then murdered, their bodies spread-eagled across the grilled windows of their plundered homes.

With vibes like those, small wonder the town is thought to be haunted. Some say the ghost is the very devil himself. I think El Demonico or "talking devil" sounds more like a mischievous poltergeist. Reports have it that he's been known to throw eggs at passersby, talk like a parrot and bombard the rooftops with stones. Some have heard the sounds of mysterious laughter, the strumming of a phantom guitar and the clicking of heels and castanets. Personally, I like that kind of devil; but apparently the local priests do not. Yes, there have been exorcisms, many of them; but they don't seem to be working.

WHERE TO STAY & WHERE TO EAT

The *Hotel El Meson del Marquez,* a delight in every respect. The two gift shops here are at least the equivalent of the best in Merida, not to mention Cancun.

The hotel itself, a survivor of the War of the Castes, is nearly 200 years old. Once the home of a Spanish marquis who got out just in time, the place was purchased in 1854 by an ancestor of the present owner, Mario Ruiz. Ruiz is a kind, thoughtful man with a sense of humor and an excellent command of English, the sort of publican one always hopes to find but rarely does. His hotel is a gem of colonial architecture as well as an oasis with its clear, clean swimming pool. One can eat in the pretty courtyard with its lush greenery, bright bougainvillaea and splashing fountain or in the well appointed dining room. The food is excellent.

Two other pleasant hotels located on the main square are the *Hotel Maria de la Luz* and *Hotel San Clemente.*

Valladolid on Highway 180 is conveniently located 60 miles west of Coba and 25 miles east of Chichen Itza. Many economy-minded travelers planning to spend time at the extensive ruins of Chichen Itza stay in Valladolid.

WHAT TO DO

• SHOPPING
If you were born to shop, as I suspect I was, this is the place. It's a paradise for collectors and bargain hunters alike.

If the ghost of John Stephens were ever to return to Valladolid, he wouldn't recognize the place. It was here that the intrepid traveler wasted precious days seeking a shoemaker. Though he'd literally walked through his soles, he was forced to move on without repairs. "There are no shoes ready made and no artist would promise to make a pair in less than a week, which I learned might be interpreted as meaning at least two," he lamented.

Today the indefatigable Stephens would find the town transformed into Sandal City. All sizes, shapes, varieties are available. The tops are covered with beautifully tooled leather, the soles are made from old tires—perfect for cleaving to the rocks, roots and reefs of the Yucatan Peninsula. These are a modern day explorers dream. Don't leave town without them.

Another Valladolid specialty are leather shoulder bags trimmed with jaguar fur. Since ancient times wearing the jaguar pelt was thought to be a means of drawing upon the creature's courage, cunning and strength—not to mention being a walking tribute to its spirit. If you don't share this atavistic bent, you can take home a bit of the jaguar's charisma in another form. Native artists carve marvelous replicas of the jungle cat—delightfully menacing creatures in all sizes with glittering green eyes and ferocious whiskers. Really charming.

Almost all the items on sale in Valladolid are indigenous to the area. Unlike much of the merchandise in major tourist areas, items are as reasonably priced as they are original and appealing. All the stores in and around the pretty plaza are worth exploring, but the Bazaar Municipal, a little arcade on the corner, is a good place to begin, particularly if time is limited.

•*CENOTES*
There's more to Valladolid than shopping. Only three blocks from the main square is the **Cenote Zaci**. A winding path meanders its way down under an immense shelf of rock overhanging the pool. Tiny, lacy-winged bats circle endlessly above the moss green water. The effect is slightly hypnotic and strangely beautiful. Adjacent to the cenote is a charming restaurant with subdued music and good food. Close by is a pretty palapa with more shopping possibilities.

Not far from the town on the road to Chichen Itza is the most beautiful cenote in Yucatan. **Dzomit** is not to be missed. Turn off at the sign. A tunnel descends to a cavern lit by a hole in the ceiling reminiscent of a Southwest Indian kiva. The water is a vibrant turquoise. Once you've slipped into those cool, incredibly clear waters you can't help but feel a sense of wonder and magic. Cenotes were always thought to be places of visions and prophecy. A dip in this one is like bathing in your own private wishing well.

Cenote Zaci

Sketch of a relic found on the Balankanche Cave

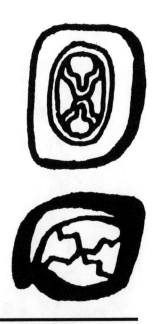

The Balankanche Caves
(bal-ann-kan-chay)

" Today, as in ancient times, the Mayans regard their caves as entrances into the underworld and avenues of communication with the gods. It's deep within the earth's inner recesses that the most sacred rituals have traditionally been performed. "

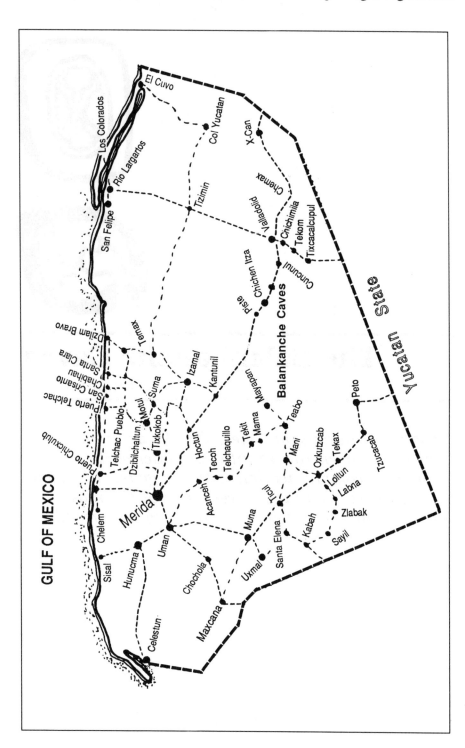

A visit to the **Balankanche Caves** is a descent into hell, but it's also an opportunity to slip into sacred space.

Today, as in ancient times, the Mayas regard their caves as entrances into the underworld and avenues of communication with the gods. It's deep within the earth's inner recesses that the most sacred rituals have traditionally been performed. Not surprisingly, their whereabouts remain a closely guarded secret whenever possible.

Balankanche (located 3 miles east of Chichen Itza on Highway 180) was no exception. Locals were extremely reluctant to open their secret ceremonial site to the public. It's easy to understand why. This place is very special.

The large network of caverns was well known to natives of the area, but no one knew—or told—just how extensive they actually were or what they contained.   Then, in 1959, Jose Humberto Gomez, a tour guide from Merida on a busman's holiday, literally stumbled into a hidden passageway which lead to an underground chamber containing an ancient shrine.

The natives were anything but happy about the discovery and warned that a curse would fall upon those who entered what they knew to be the secret retreat of the rain god, Chac. But the eager archaeologists who quickly converged on the area were not about to be dissuaded. Finally the apprehensive priests decided to conduct a ceremony of appeasement.

Thirteen priests and a small group of children gathered for an all-night rite barred to outsiders. Then in an ancient, but obviously well remembered ritual, animals were sacrificed as Chac's forgiveness was sought for allowing his sanctuary to be profaned by archaeologists and the inevitable visitors who would follow. It would appear that the rain god heard their entreaties and was moved. An unseasonable down pour followed drenching the parched countryside.

Today the Balankanche Caves are open for viewing. A guide unlocks the iron gate that prevents curiosity seekers from roaming at will. Only a few people seek out the caves and that's probably just as well. It takes time to navigate the narrow, steep passageways.

Inside the air is damp and earthy, the dimness a startling contrast to the dazzling sunshine outside. Visitors must de-scend single file as the outside light recedes until it's gone completely. From that point the cramped passageway is lit only by faint–very faint–bulbs suspended from the ceiling.

Finally the tunnel snakes its way past a cenote so clear that it resembles a canyon. In the center, surrounded by water, an image of Chac watches from atop a rough altar. The ceiling is low in places, the ground damp and often uneven. The caverns seem to close in, the effect is eerie, uncomfortable, too far removed from the sunburst outside. And then, at last, the winding maze emerges from the gloom into the ceremonial chamber.

It's immediately obvious why Balankanche means "Throne of the Jaguar" (priest) or the "Hidden Treasure of the Jaguar." Both names are apt. There's a vast array of treasure and a kind of throne in the shape of a magnificent tree formed by a stalactite joined to a stalagmite with thousands of tiny stalactites projecting from the ceiling like leaves. This, the ancients believed, represented the sacred ceiba tree, the Tree of Life, directly connected with their fertility rituals.

Flanking the entranceway are two censors for burning copal. Around the altar-tree are hundreds of ceremonial vessels, spindle whorls and grinding stones positioned exactly as the priests left them; and, unlike artifacts of like vintage exposed for centuries to the sun, these retain their original color.

The effect is overwhelming, the reaction one of awe coupled with a nagging suspicion that somewhere not too far away the old gods still live.

Temple of Kukulkan – Chichen Itza

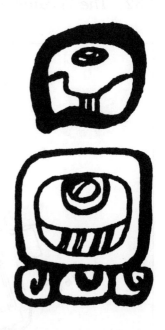

Chichen Itza
(chee-chen-eet-sa)

"Chichen Itza was not only a ceremonial center but a commercial one. It's easy to forget that this monument of cold stone and lost memories was once thronged with vendors hawking condiments, vegetables, jewels and slaves. It's hard to imagine cages of barkless, hairless edible dogs, brightly plumaged birds talking Maya and chattering monkeys, yet we know they existed. There would also have been areas set aside for feather merchants, goldsmiths, curanderos or healers, scribes and story tellers. "

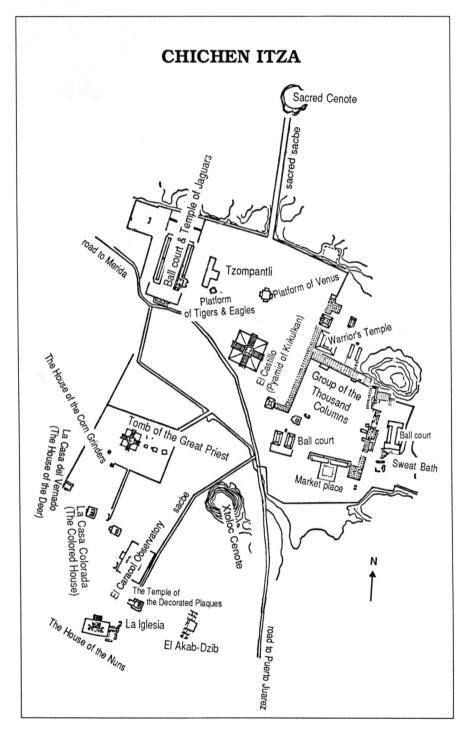

CHICHEN ITZA

Sacred Cenote

sacred sacbe

Ball court & Temple of Jaguars

road to Merida

Tzompantli

Platform of Venus

Platform of Tigers & Eagles

El Castillo (Pyramid of Kukulkan)

Warrior's Temple

Group of the Thousand Columns

The House of the Corn Grinders

La Casa del Venado (The House of the Deer)

Tomb of the Great Priest

Ball court

Ball court

Sweat Bath

Market place

La Casa Colorada (The Colored House)

sacbe

Xtoloc Cenote

El Caracol Observatory

The Temple of the Decorated Plaques

La Iglesia

El Akab-Dzib

The House of the Nuns

road to Puerto Juarez

N

W hat was I doing alone in a jungle in the middle of the night? It was a good question, frequently repeated.

First there'd been a ritual ceremony remininisent of long ago days as a Camp Fire Girl, not a peak experience by any means. Afterwards the others in our group had scattered, most returning to the hotel. Departing with them were the two Mayan guides who'd led us to this isolated spot in Old Chichen. *They* weren't about to spend a night out in the brush far from their homes and hammocks. Neither was our intrepid leader who'd planned this "alone time" in the wilderness.

"My body tells me I should go back," she announced shortly after the chanting and incense burning had ended. (My body would have, too, if accompanied by her new boy friend.)

The ground was hard, lumpy. After a hot steamy day, the night was surprisingly cold. The two blankets I'd smuggled out of the Mayaland Hotel were totally inadequate and so was my light sweater. I thought wistfully of the Mayan guides and particularly of their machetes as I listened to the strange rustling noises all around me . Then I thought of bats, vampire bats. I thought of tarantulas and other more poisonous spiders, some I'd been told were the size of golf balls. I thought of scorpions, of slithering snakes, of prowling jaguars. I didn't have to think of insects. I felt them.

I recalled a story heard only the day before. A photographer had wandered off the trail. When at last a search party found him, all that was left was a skeleton, a camera and the money in his pockets. But that was in Guatemala, not Chichen Itza, I reminded myself, more than once.

Tourists rarely go to Old Chichen. It's well off the beaten track. This was new country to me, the hotel a good two miles away. Trying to mentally retrace my steps, I recalled the overgrown path that led through dense brush. Could I find my way back? My flashlight flickered ominously, dimmed, then gave out completely. I scrapped that idea.

The overnight had been suggested as a vision quest. The Indians, who are big on such things, feel that animal contact is an important part of the ritual. It's supposed to be a very meaningful experience. I hoped fervently that my quest wouldn't include a meaningful experience with a wild boar.

It was going to be a very long night. I tried to relax, seeking a soothing pattern in the rustling leaves. It was cold and I was tired, very, very tired. And then quite suddenly a form appeared. It was a woman. I could see her quite clearly in the moonlight She was dressed in a white blouse with a little tie and brown pants tucked into high boots. The hair peeking below a pith helmet was bobbed.

"I'm glad you finally made it," she said to me. "I remember you as a little girl who liked to read about the Mayas and longed to be an archaeologist.   It's good that you came, you've a job to do here."

I looked at her in amazement, a vague memory faintly stirring.   A children's book long, long ago. The writer a young woman archaeologist. I'd idolized her.

"The jungle *is* a little scary at first," she admitted. "I was afraid in the beginning too. But nothing will harm you, I promise. Why don't you just go to sleep."

And, surprisingly, I did.   A month later, home in

California, I was able to locate with much effort the book I'd read as a child, *Digging In Yucatan*. There was a picture inside of the pretty author, Ann Axtell Morris. She was dressed as I'd seen her that night in the jungle. What a trickster the subconscious can be. Was it a vision or "merely" a dream? And does it really matter?

The night was an empowering experience, one that brought many aspects of my life into sharper focus. Would I do it again? Probably not. It was a crazy thing to do. Would I trade a million dollars for the memory? Absolutely not!

As for the work that Ann spoke of–my task?
Perhaps this book is it.

Some people resent what they view as the "commercialism" of Chichen Itza. They're openly disdainful of the colorful clotheslines strung with T-shirts and dresses, the family groupings selling onyx chess sets, carvings, etc. Personally, I rather like all this hustle. It seems very appropriate since Ek Chuah, the Mayan god of trade, was one of the deities highly venerated here.

Chichen Itza was not only a ceremonial center but a commercial one. It's easy to forget that this monument of cold stone and lost memories was once thronged with vendors hawking condiments, vegetables, jewels and slaves. It's hard to imagine cages of barkless, hairless edible dogs, brightly plumaged birds talking Mayan and chattering monkeys, yet we know they existed. There would also have been areas set aside for feather merchants, goldsmiths, *curanderos* or healers, scribes and story tellers.

Too bad that none of the latter are around to tell us what really happened here. We know very little, for this—the most famous of all the Mayan cities—was found in an abandoned state.   Chichen Itza, which means mouth of the well of the Itza or possibly wizard—since the Itzas were credited with being wizards—flourished during the classic period from 300 to 900 AD. It's believed to have been abandoned, then reinhabited around 1000 AD under Toltec domination.

Jaguar crawl – Temple of Kukulkan

The synthesis of Toltec and Maya is clearly evident. Quetzalcoatl, the feathered serpent deity, was revered by both the Toltecs and the Aztecs (who probably pushed the Toltecs out of central Mexico into Yucatan.) Representations of this deity—now known as Kukulcan—are seen throughout the site. We also see the Mexican eagle joining the Mayan jaguar on wall carvings. Obviously the old Mayan order had been overthrown, but Mayan priests and noblemen were incorporated into the new establishment. Then, unaccountably, Chichen Itza was abandoned once again in 1250 A.D. —300 years before the arrival of the Spaniards– though it continued to be the site of religious pilgrimages until after the conquest.

Excavations have been going on for more than 100 years, yet archaeologists can still only speculate about what happened here. Only the stones know the true secrets of the Mayas, the Itzas or the Toltecs whose cultures are layered in the ruins that visitors see today. The cleared and restored portion of the city is about two miles square, yet it may represent only five percent of the total. South of the road that bisects the site is "old" Chichen Itza where surviving buildings date from 600 to 900 A.D. "New" Chichen Itza, north of the road, was built from 1000 to 1250 A.D.

Today the majestic stone pyramids, temples and palaces towering above the jungle-covered plane hold the same fascination for tourists as they did for the conquistadores more than 400 years ago.

One of the first tourists, John L. Stephens, literally put Chichen Itza on the map with his lucid travel writing. His account, written in 1842, still captures the magic of the **Well of Sacrifice** for which the city was named:

"...setting out from the Castillo, at some distance we ascended a wooded elevation, which seemed an artificial causeway leading to the cenote. The cenote was the largest and wildest we had seen; in the midst of a thick forest, an immense circular hole, with cragged perpendicular sides, trees growing out of them and overhanging the brink, and still as if the genius of consummate silence reigned within. A hawk was sailing around it, looking down into the water, but without flapping its wings. The water was of a greenish hue. A mysterious influence seemed to pervade it, in unison with the historical account that the well of Chichen was a place of pilgrimage, and that human victims were thrown into it in sacrifice. In one place on the very brink, were the remains of a stone structure, probably connected with ancient superstitious rites; perhaps the place from which victims were thrown into the dark well beneath."

It was this well, also known as the **Sacred Cenote,** which gave the site its ceremonial significance. The life-sustaining power of water was all important to the Mayas, the cenote–a natural well–a gift from the gods. But sometimes it was necessary to propitiate those gods. Human beings–most frequently women–as well as jewels and ornaments were frequently hurled into the well.

On rare occasions, the victims flung into the jade green depths of the pool survived; and, when they returned to the surface, they were thought to bring with them messages from the gods.

Hunac Ceel, a consummate risk taker and opportunist, used this precarious vehicle to rise from commoner to king. Here was a volunteer victim who not only survived but brought back a prophecy about a new monarch–himself. What could the priests do with a man so divinely inspired but fulfill his destiny?

Edward H. Thompson, some 800 years later, seems to have been cut from the same cloth. He, too, was fated to make waves in the sacred well. Thompson, while still a student at Worcester Polytechnic Institute, wrote an article entitled, "Atlantis Not a Myth," which appeared in *Popular Science Monthly*. His premise, that the mysterious Mayan civilization on the Yucatan Peninsula might be a branch of the lost continent of Atlantis, won him friends in high places.

Stephen Salisbury, one of the founders of the American Antiquarian Society, and Charles P. Bowditch, the guiding light of the Peabody Museum of Anthropology, functioned much like high priests. They agreed that Thompson was the very man to investigate Yucatan, an area that had long fascinated both. With one fell swoop, they insured him both a free hand and a salary by using their political influence to get him appointed U.S. Consul to Yucatan and Campeche. In 1885, Thompson–the youngest consul in U.S. history–set off with his wife and baby daughter to explore Yucatan. It was an adventure that would occupy the next forty years of his life.

Five years later Thompson was able to send a vast array of temple molds for display at the 1890 Chicago World's Fair. Allison V. Armour, the meat magnate, was so impressed that he made Thompson a cash gift that enabled him to purchase the ruins of Chichen Itza. For about $75, the young consul acquired nearly 100 square miles of land which included a Spanish plantation house dating from the 1700's and untold acres of ruins. At that time the outpost area was accessible only by a jungle footpath. On the night he took possession of the place, Thompson stumbled over the remains of the last inhabitant of his new hacienda who'd been murdered by insurrectionists.

Undaunted, Thompson settled in and turned his attention to the legendary cenote. This was and is an oval-shaped opening in the rocky earth crust with a diameter of 180 feet and craggy sides which fall abruptly 60 feet to the rim of the water. Far below the dark green surface is a layer of mud.

Like Hunac Ceel, Thompson had a dream that lured him into that mud. In 1579 the mayor of nearby Valladolid had written to Charles V, "The lords and principal personages of the land had the custom, after sixty days of abstinence and fast-ing, of arriving by daybreak at the mouth of the Cenote and throwing into it Indian women belonging to each of these lords and personages, at the same time telling these women to ask for their masters a year favorable to their particular needs and desires."

A few women were said to have survived the ordeal. At noon, those that still could, cried out and were pulled up by means of ropes. These survivors told strange tales. Many people of their nation dwelled beneath the waters. These men and women greeted them with heavy blows when they tried to raise their heads. When the victims heads were turned downward they saw "many deeps and hollows, and they the people, responded to their queries concerning the good or bad year that was in store for their masters."

Of less melodrama and more interest to Thompson was mention of treasure being thrown into the sacred well along with the maidens.

Thompson made friends with the *H'Menes* , or Mayan wisemen, who initiated him into the *Sh'Tol Brothers,* a sacred society that had escaped the Spaniards. The *H'Menes* confirmed the legend and pointed out to him the area of the cenote beneath which the rain god had his palace.

It remained only for Thompson to take the plunge. Holding a torch with a submarine telephone in one hand, the young archaeologist shook hands with the other. Then he was lowered to the cenote surface on a pontoon from which he dove into the depth. Feeling only slightly more secure than the sacrificial victims, Thompson groped his way down sixty feet into the ooze. Though his diving gear may have been considered state of the art for 1904, it was still very primitive. One must marvel at courage only slightly less than Hunac Ceel's. Several of these early dives were very nearly fatal; one resulted in a ruptured eardrum.

Day after day passed, then week after week. Once Thompson floated up to the surface by accident without warning and struck the bottom of the pontoon with a loud thump. His terrified helpers ran off screaming, certain that it was Chac rising in righteous anger at this invasion of his sacred sanctum. Load after load of mud was brought up and examined. Hours of heartbreaking anxiety and backbreaking efforts netted nothing more than rotting leaves, decayed twigs and fallen trees.

Then one day two white balls of something turned up in the muck. Thompson pounced on them, felt them, smelled them, tore one open and touched a match to its heart. As a long spiral of sweet-scented smoke curled upward, he recalled the words of one of the *H' Men:*
"In ancient times our fathers burned the sacred resin and by the fragrant smoke their prayers were wafted to their god whose home was in the sun."

Thompson shouted and

Cenote – Chichen Itza

• •
─────
•

danced like a child, realizing that the two small balls were copal which the Mayas used for incense. For him, it was the scent of victory. He knew now that he was close. A few days later he raised the skeletons of three women. Soon after gold discs were uncovered, then jade, precious ornaments, jewelry–hundreds of priceless artifacts of all kinds. Most of these relics were discreetly smuggled out of the country to his Boston sponsors.

So there was Hunac Ceel diving into the Well of Sacrifice in search of fame and fortune, followed by Edward Thompson hoping to extract a bit of the same. Unfortunately Thompson wasn't as lucky as his predecessor. Success was followed by disaster. An ill advised article on his archaeological finds in the New York *Times* reached the eyes of the Mexican authorities who promptly slapped a million peso lien on Thompson's Chichen Itza property.

In the midst of the ensuring litigation, a local revolution erupted, and his hacienda was burned by rebels, the crops destroyed and cattle driven off. The most tragic loss was Thompson's priceless library. "Much of the fruit of my long life of studies went up in a whirlwind of smoke and ashes," he wrote out of the depth of his depression. It was a crushing blow; but Thompson, now well into his sixties, rallied.

In an effort to recoup some of his losses, he rebuilt the hacienda, hoping to turn it into a hotel. The idea was later realized by others, but at the time Thompson's legal and financial difficulties made it impossible. Eventually a deal was struck whereby the Carnegie Institution took over the hacienda and continued his work. Disheartened, the explorer of the the Well of Sacrifice left the only home of his adult life and his beloved ruins, returning to the United States.

⋮⋮

More recent dives with modern equipment have netted startling findings. According to legend, the victims were virgins. This fine point can't be determined, but it does seem certain that at least some of the women didn't go willingly. Heads showed evidence of severe blows and one woman suffered a fractured nose. This new evidence also calls to mind the enigmatic story of the pugilistic people who dwell beneath the waters.

The peak of the sacrificial cult was reached after the decline of Toltec Chichen (by 1250 AD) and continued beyond Colonial times–far beyond. A doll was hauled up from the depth wrapped in *rayon* cloth.

Today one approaches the cenote by way of the T-shirt trail, bright offerings all along the way; but once beyond, the chatter stops. The well has changed little since Thompson's day–or Hunac Ceel's for that matter. Visitors almost tiptoe to the edge, gaze wonderingly into the murky depths with a sort of fearful curiosity, then draw back to talk in instinctively lowered tones. A sense of mystery, even of horror, pervades, surviving the lapse of centuries.

The most impressive and intriguing structure in Chichen Itza is the **Temple of Kukulkan**, sometimes referred to as **El Castillo** because the Spanish conquistador, Francisco de Montejo set up his headquarters there. Whatever one calls it, this construction is as fascinating for architects as it is to archaeologists and astronomers. It took Frank Lloyd Wright, whose revolutionary use of geometric form in architectural design was generations ahead of his time, to point out the perspective of each of the staircases. As you face them head-on, they appear as wide at the top as at the bottom. Looking more carefully, it becomes apparent that the steps widen gradually, giving the illusion of symmetry as they get farther away.

That isn't all. Besides being an architectural triumph, the Temple of Kukulcan is a kind of time machine.

First of all there are four stairways (four creatures held up the world) with 91 steps, comprising a total of 364; plus a platform which totals 365—as in days of the year. The 52 panels on each side represent the 52-year cycle of the Mayan calendar (the Calendar Round) with nine terraces (nine regions of the Mayan underworld) on each side of the stairways— a total of 18 terraces to represent the 18-month ceremonial calendar.

————————— **The Road to Life–*The Mayan Calendar*** —————————

In a world regulated by clock radios, parking meters and time tables, it's difficult to understand the Mayan fascination with the slow, dignified ritual progression of long periods of time.

This was a system of cycles moving within cycles in an endlessly rotating wheel. "Progress," as we know it, had no part in it. Not surprisingly, the Mayans were fatalists. The movements of the heavenly bodies weren't thought of as revolutions but as events that repeated themselves in a given pattern as time itself was repeating. It's as if all the secrets of the universe were contained in these calculations with the lives of the Mayan people rigidly governed by calendars and their portents.

The Mayan scientists, often mind boggling in their brilliance, had little interest in pure science for its own sake. Astronomy and mathematics were merely a means of divination and regulation of religious ritual. When the Mayans recorded their his-

tory they also foretold the future in terms of the past. In putting
together astronomical calculations and ritual cycles, they developed the most sophisticated calendar in history.   The ancient
Greeks had *something* like it. They called it the "zodiac," or
road of life.

First there was **The Solar Calendar**, which was precisely measured and consisted of 365.24 days. This was a measure of eight-
een "months" of twenty days
plus an extra five. Those five
days weren't really considered
days, but rather a necessary
gap between one year's last
month and the next year's
first. At this season the sun
was generally pale and cool
and hung low in the sky. It
was thought that the gods
dozed and no sensible person

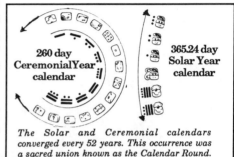

The Solar and Ceremonial calendars
converged every 52 years. This occurrence was
a sacred union known as the Calendar Round.

would do anything to risk annoyance by disturbing them.

During these five "lifeless" days it was considered fruitless, even
rash or hazardous to do anything.   All avoidable activities
ceased.   Couples refrained from sexual connections less they
conceive a child and children born during this period were considered highly unlucky. Crowds were avoided, cooking fires extinguished; people stayed indoors, occupying themselves with
trivial pursuits such as mending fish nets or tools. Mostly they
sat about contemplating the awful possibility that the world
might end at any moment.

The days of the month in this secular calendar are numbered O
Pop, 1 Pop, 2 Pop, etc.,through 19 Pop, when one then goes on to
the next month.

The Ceremonial Calendar, completely different from the solar
one, operated concurrently. It, too, had twenty days, each with
a definite character, some auspicious, others malevolent. All
were named for gods, beginning with Imix, the earth god.
These days were attached to numbers, 1 through 13. At the end
of the 13th day, the numbers started anew. In this way 260 days—
13 times 20—passed before the same name was again accompanied by the same number. (Imix and 1, for instance.)

Priest-historians used this calendar for recording such significant events as wars, the length of a ruler's reign and– most importantly– foretelling the future. This was divinatory almanac or *Book of Good and Bad Days* , a *Book of Fate* rather than a calendar dependent on seasons. The primary function of priests was to be the guardians of this astronomical and calendrical data, using it to propitiate the gods, to tell the people when to cut and burn their fields, to plant and to celebrate.

The sacred and secular calendars mesh, so that a significant day can be read today on a stela– such as 2 Imix, 4 Pop. The two calendars, one with a cycle of 365.24 days and the other with 260, converge every 52 years. This occurrence was a sacred union known as the **Calendar Round.** For most, it was a once in a lifetime experience.

The Observatory – Chichen Itza

To these calendars was added a third, **The Venus Calendar,** based on the transits of the planet Venus. Sometimes Venus served as the after blossom that blazed immediately after sunset. At other times it moved on to the other side of the sky where it would be the last star visible as the sun rose and washed away all the others. Lovely as all this star-talk sounds, astroarchaeologists now believe that the Venus transits and calendar data had a direct bearing on war strategy.

And yes, the Venus Calendar was also linked to the other two. The length of the Venus synodical revolution in the heavens varies between 580 and 588 days over a span of five revolutions, giving an average length of 583.92 days. The Mayans made it 584 so that five Venus "years" equated with eight solar years of 365 days. The discrepancy between 584 and the actual length of the Venus revolution was made up by corrections amounting to 24 days in the course of 301 revolutions, which reduced to an error of one day in every 6000 years. These machinations were necessary to also reconcile the Venus Calendar with the ceremonial one.

Convoluted as all this sounds, the Mayan chronological system based on names and numbers for days and months enabled the priests to designate a particular date which could not be mistaken for any other through thousands of years.

And here's one more bit of intrigue to ponder. This complex system is known to have begun on August 12, 3113 BC. This cycle—in which we are currently living—will end, if the Mayan priests are correct, with the destruction of the world on December 24, 2011.

The pyramid was built over an earlier structure undoubtedly at the end of some long ago 52-year cycle. Inside, a narrow, claustrophobic stairway ascends to a sacrificial altar-throne encrusted with jade—thought to be Chinese in origin. How did it get there?

Equally intriguing is the shadow of a giant snake which descends from the Temple of Kukulkan twice a year—always at the spring and fall equinoxes. On the 21st of March and again on the 21st of September, the shadowy reptile slithers its way along the balustrade disappearing in the direction of the sacred cenote just as the sun sets. For 34 minutes, the snake created by a play of light and shadow moves from the top of the pyramid to its base. For the ancients it must have been the ultimate fertility symbol. The golden sun god had penetrated the earth. It was time to plant.

Dr. Clemency Coggins of the Peabody Museum at Harvard University believes that the pyramid and the snake were the core of a new ceremonial center established in Chichen Itza to mark the year 830 AD which united the Mayas with the Toltec arrivals from central Mexico. This was the year, she believes, that a major Mayan time period ended, and the year when the Toltecs had to rekindle their fires.

The new fire ritual took place every 52 years.   To commemorate the occasion a captive was sacrificed, and a new fire kindled in the victim's recently vacated heart cavity. Such measures were necessary in order to prevent the sun from abandoning the earth completely. Both priest and peasant knew that the sun required nourishment to remain strong and diligent in its daily labors. What could be more re-vitalizing than the very life energy the sun itself gave? It all makes perfect sense, except whatever happened to Kukulcan's original message of peace?

The ruling priests would undoubtedly have marked the approach of this sacred date decades in advance and planned the new ceremonial center to commemorate it. Coggins speculates that the pyramid would have been completed the previous year, so that the serpent's shadow would move down the stairway for the first time on March 21, 830.

The genius that made this magic trick possible was fostered on the other side of Chichen Itza in a building called **El Caracol** by the Spaniards. The "snail" name comes from its twisting interior staircase. The building is now known to have been an observatory–the only one in Mayaland. It is the oldest Toltec building on the site and the greatest achievement.

The circular superstructure consists of a lower story with radial shafts emerging from its center. The platforms, doorways and shafts were aligned in accordance with the cycles of the Sun, the stars, and the planet Venus.

It's no simple matter to make accurate observations of sunrises and sunsets, eclipses, and planetary transits in a country of frequent tropical rainfalls, yet that's exactly what was going on in this extraordinary building. Night after night Mayan priests using only their eyes marked the heavens with remarkable sophistication. They were particularly fascinated by the planet Venus.

Limited by what they could see, the Mayas had no idea of the solar system's planets revolving around the sun, but they knew that Venus appeared and disappeared on the western and eastern horizons at different times of the year and that it took 584 days to complete the cycle. They also knew, as has been previously explained, that five of these Venus cycles equaled eight solar years. Venus, then, appeared at northerly and southerly extremes every eight years. Several aspects of El Caracol's alignments point to these southerly and northerly Venus extremes. The Venus combinations come up again and again in Mayan almanacs or astrological handbooks indicating that this planet had a role in all aspects of Mayan life.

Obviously the Mayan priests were well rewarded for their brilliance. The rich ceremonial life of the people centered around their calendars and observations. Imagine the effect upon the people when the priests predicted an eclipse and that eclipse occurred on schedule. Imagine the power of one who contained all the secrets of the universe in his calculations.

Here was a science that sought to explain and connect every

aspect of human affairs, relating celestial movements to war, agriculture, politics and environment. To write it off because of the nontechnological basis or the astrological/religious roots would be shortsighted. This was a science that developed in an environment devoid of technology, and this was a science that worked.

Nothing comparable to the magnificent **Temple of the Warriors** has ever been found in America. When archaeologists happened on it in 1924, there was only a great mound thickly covered with thorn bushes. Tops of columns showed above the tangle, many more lay sprawling in the thick brambles. The archaeologists began to count them—800, 900; then just before rounding back to the starting place, the grand total of 1000. And so the place received the other name for which it is frequently known, **The Temple of the Thousand Columns.**

It would take them four years of excavation to lay bare the vast complex of buildings piled upon buildings, pyramids within pyramids, hidden paintings, grotesque sculpture, buried sacrificial treasure and tunneled passages. In the midst of a series of major and minor revolutions, with admitted bandidos for workmen, the archaeological team preceded to uncover and restore one of the most impressive and beautiful structures anywhere in the world.

Today the approach through impressive files of square columns is like a huge foyer. Each colonnade is decorated on all four faces with reliefs of Toltec officers. Originally their eyes were inlaid with white shells, the pupils painted in pitch—consider the effect. These stone colonnades originally constituted the sub-structure of the temple and helped hold up the heavy beamed roofs that collapsed long ago.

Inside is a pyramid with four terraces rising to a height of 37 feet. Two statues of standard bearers guard the top of the stairs leading to the last terrace where Chac-Mool gazes out upon the main plaza. This is a stony reminder that countless numbers of sacrificial victims died on a nearby altar, bodies arched backwards, chests thrust forward as if

The Temple of a Thousand Columns

eager for the blade. Here the priest sliced open the chest of the victim, tearing loose the still beating heart from its enlargement of blood vessels. It was thought that the heart donor lived long enough to see his still throbbing heart held triumphantly aloft by the priest, then placed in Chac Mool's sacred basin. It was also believed that sacrificial victims— as well as women who died in childbirth—lived out their afterlives in a very special paradise.

The entrance to the temple itself is flanked by two feathered serpents and beyond them is the principal sanctuary with its altar supported by Atlantean Toltec warriors. All interior walls had been frescoed with lively scenes related to the Toltec conquest of Yucatan. Intriguingly, some of the Mayas are pictured with blond hair.

After two years of excavations–when the end of their labors seemed in sight–the archaeologists discovered the vestiges of still another structure, now called the **Temple of Chac-Mool**. This one seems to have been almost a model for the later more impressive structure. Among the rubble the remains of a giant Chac-Mool was found, which must once have towered above the temple entrance in awesome grandeur.

Architecturally at least, Chichen Itza went out with a bang, not a whimper. Built in 1250 A.D., The Temple of the Warriors was very likely the last building constructed, an eloquent final statement.

The saying, "Good guys don't win ball games," could very well have originated in Chichen Itza, where ball teams literally played for keeps. Most Mayan ceremonial centers had ball courts, but the "Olympics" –the Mayan Ball Games were well established in the New World about 500 years before the Greeks founded the Olympic Games during the first century B.C.– must have been played on the gigantic **Sacred Ballcourt** opposite the Temple of the Warriors.

The playing field proper is 309 feet long and 114 feet wide. Two walls 26 feet high flank its entire length. At the field's center two large stone hoops are positioned near the top of each wall–23 feet above the ground. Spectators sat on the two long terraces that run along the base of the walls.

This was a savage, ritualistic game played with knees, hips

and elbows. The use of hands and feet was against the rules. The idea was to get the rubber ball through the stone hoops—obviously a rare occurrence. The winning team was far more apt to be the one that committed the fewest errors: touching the ball with the hands, allowing it to touch the ground or go out of bounds.

On the night before the game, the two teams prayed. Players asked the gods for blessings for themselves and their equipment (helmets, kneepads, shoulderpads, mallets.) There's no question that they needed all the help they could get. The bas-reliefs bordering the eastern terrace below the great stone serpent are grimly explicit. Seven

Bas-reliefs of victors – next to the Ball Park, Chichen Itza

players of each team are shown gathered around a ball decorated with a human skull. Two large spirals rise out of the skull's jaws symbolizing death.

In the central scene the first player on the team holds in his right hand a sacrificial knife; in his left hand is the head of the presumed captain of the opposing team, the losers. The torso of the decapitated man is on its knees, and from his bleeding neck seven serpents writhe–the central snake in the shape of a luxuriant plant full of flowers and fruit.

Here we have seven players, seven serpents. The number seven symbolized maize–life itself to the Mayas. In some way this, too, must have been a fertility sacrifice. The ball perhaps represented the course of the sun, with the result of the match, or the sacrifice involved, fertilizing the earth. Very likely the winning team carried out prescribed rituals involving the use of the losing group as sacrificial victims.

Whatever the rationale, the heads of the losers adorned the rack on the adjoining skull platform, or *Tzompantli*. Carvings of skulls encircle the platform today. Another interesting bas-relief adjacent to the ball court is a reminder that this grisly stuff was the gift of the conquering Toltecs. It shows the Toltec eagle holding a sacrificial heart, positioned next to the Mayan jaguar now also doing the same. The inference being the acceptance of a new, more militaristic culture.

Did you see *Against All Odds*? If not, the local guides will be more than happy to fill you in on a plot that was steamy in more ways than one. Jeff Bridges and Rachel Ward got into the sensuous mood of Chichen Itza when they retired to the **Sweat Baths** for a torrid love scene. (A rerun of this movie on your VCR does give an amusing, if slightly skewered view of the site.)

Perhaps the Sweat Baths were once used for ceremonial purposes–possibly by the ball players. Today one can see the remains of a waiting room, a steam room, the oven and underground drainage canals.

Among the most intricate and beautiful carvings at the site are those found on the walls of the **Nunnery,** an excellent example of Late Classic architecture. The original purpose of the Nunnery is unknown, but the Spaniards put it to practical use during the conquest.

The Mayas put up a stiff fight for their sacred city, forcing the Spaniards back until they finally sought refuge in the tower atop the Nunnery. At first this seemed good strategy. The foundation of the building was high with straight walls and staircases so steep that it seemed a simple matter to defend the building from attack.

The Mayas agreed, so they simply fell back. No fight, no contest. Theirs would be a waiting game. Sooner or later the Spaniards would need a drink of water badly enough to come down and get it.

Before long the Spaniards did get thirsty, and hungry too. Finally there was only a little food left. That night their leader played a desperate game with it. A hungry Mayan dog was lured up the stairs with offers of meat, then grabbed and tied to a bell. Meat was placed all around him just beyond reach. All night long the dog pulled in one direction then another, setting off a frantic clamor.

Thinking this signified an attack, the Mayas massed around the stairway and readied themselves for battle. The noise continued all night long. When dawn broke the Mayas began to cautiously ascend the stairs. At the top they found a deserted fort held only by their own miserable dog. The Spaniards had all escaped by sliding down a rope on the back side of the building.

The Nunnery had another use in the 1880's when the English scholar, Alfred Maudslay, camped out there. Maudslay and his companion, Miss Annie Hunter, had hardly arrived before they each came down with malaria. A peculiarity of the disease is that it frequently strikes on alternate days. On one day the patient may have a high fever, while on the next he's tired but normal. As it turned out, Alfred and Annie were afflicted on opposite days, so they were able to care for each other in shifts. It couldn't have been easy, the nearest water was a mile round trip up and down a precarious trail. Somehow the intrepid team put in six months in this fashion, all the while mapping, drawing and photographing the ruins.

Another remarkable pair were Alice and Augustis Le Plongeon, who despite a revolution going on around them, took more than 500 photographs of Chichen Itza and made 20 careful sheets of mural drawings. The couple ventured deep into the jungle, encountering natives who practiced mesmerism, induced clairvoyance, and used "magic mirrors" to predict the future.

From a 150-year old Maya, Le Plongeon learned that men still existed who could decipher some of mysterious hieroglyphs scattered about the area. As he himself mastered these hieroglyphs, Le Plongeon came to believe that a strong link existed between the Mayas and the lost continent of Atlantis.

More practically, he was the first of the archaeologists to

sense that the Mayas might be building one pyramid on top of the other. There was only one way to prove his hunch. It was drastic, but Le Plongeon bit the bullet–almost literally. He dynamited the building, only to reveal yet another hidden within. Today you can see evidence of his daring, which paved the way for other more sophisticated means of exploration.

There are many more smaller, but equally interesting buildings waiting to be explored. Some are mere piles of rock and stone crying out for rescue from the death grip of the jungle. These are located in the area known as **Old Chichen.**

To reach them, continue down the road to the south, away from the main ruins and past the Hotel Hacienda Chichen, the original hacienda which Edward Thompson once bought for $75. Follow the trail to the right. It isn't well marked, but that adds to the adventure. Most who venture here agree that the experience is worth the effort. After a half hour or so with the madding crowd far behind, you begin to have some sense of the mystery that has drawn so many explorers to this remarkable area.

Soon you'll see two Atlantean figures supporting a door lintel which contains a hieroglyphic of the year 879 A.D., the only proven date in Chichen Itza. Beyond this is the **Temple of the Phalli.** The unknown sculptor of the objects protruding from the temple walls leaves little doubt about what he had in mind. Since, as a rule, the Mayas didn't go in for erotic art, it's believed that this was a temple dedicated to fertility. Some believe that couples who wished to have children may have come to this sanctuary.

Other temples reclaimed by jungle include the **Temple of the Little Heads, Temple of the Four Lintels, Temple of the Jaguar, Temple of the Turtle,** and **Temple of the Sculptured Door Jambs.** All are named for the remnants of carvings found on the walls, or for outstanding architectural features. All about you is verdant jungle for unbroken miles.   Continuing on through the brush, you'll come to two Atlantean columns beneath which this writer spent one very long night.

The Atlantean Columns

WHERE TO STAY

No matter what the season, Chichen Itza will be hot at midday. This is the time to enjoy a leisurely margarita or splash in a pool, not clamber up pyramids. It's best to plan on spending *at least* one night at Chichen Itza. This will enable you to explore in the morning when it's cool and in the late afternoon when the Sun God turns benevolent showering the temples with burnished gold.

There are any number of tours that can arrange this for you, or you can rent a car or hop a bus in Merida. Once at Chichen Itza, there are three hotel possibilities immediately adjacent to the ruins.

Hotel Hacienda Chichen would be the most interesting, assuming that it's open. Edward Thompson's explorations were made from here and some of the Mayan stones were used in the hacienda construction. Each cottage is named for an early archaeologist who worked at Chichen. The narrow-gauge railroad tracks used in the 1920s for transportation and hauling still go through the grounds. This place is charming, has all the amenities; but has been closed lately. One more Mayan mystery.

Hotel Mayaland is a very close second. The building, begun in 1922, somehow manages to blend colonial architecture with art deco. The high ceilings, tile floors, heavy mahogany furniture, wooden louvered windows, inlaid door jambs and lintels are reminiscent of some exotic movie. The grounds, literally a botanical garden, are dotted with cottages built like Mayan bungalows with thatched roofs. Inside one sleeps under mosquito netting, but in a real bed—not a hammock. The furniture is massive, exquisitely carved, once again a movie set feeling. Not surprisingly, the place *is* a favorite of film stars— as well as presidents, dictators, and royalty. (A thank you note from Lyndon Johnson hangs in the gift shop.) Don't miss the magnificent mural of the creation myth in the dining room.

Hotel Villa Arqueologica is the new kid on the block with clean, classy, state of the art amenities. Though run by the Club Med, don't expect a landlocked Love Boat. This place is *quiet*. Oh, well, you need your energy for climbing pyramids.

Since all three fall into the medium price bracket, they very well could be full. Two others to consider in nearby Piste are *Hotel Mision Chichen Itza* and the *Pyramid Inn*. Both are clean, comfortable, well appointed and slightly cheaper.

Thompson's Hacienda is now the Hotel Hacienda

WHERE TO EAT

You go to Chichen Itza to get into the ambience of the ruins and the country and that's about it. All the hotels have restaurants with adequate to excellent food—depending on who's in the kitchen at the time. Each hotel has an attractive shop. There are also a few "curio" stores in Piste and a number of restaurants to sample. A guide recommended his brother-in-law's restaurant, insisting that it was the best in town. I thought "Oh, sure it is," but was glad I tried it. He was right, it is! Try *Restaurant Xaybe.* Another one of those "X-words", it's pronounced shabe.

WHAT TO DO

Night time entertainment narrows down to the *Sound and Light Show* which is presented twice nightly (the effects are often spectacular), or strolling about Piste where there are always promenaders and often dancers in the square. Cap either with a bit of stargazing. After all, that's what Chichen Itza is all about.

Merida – the white city

Merida
(may-ree-dah)

"Merida has a very special flavor totally unlike any other city in Mexico. One could easily spend hours people watching while sitting on one of the lacy, wrought iron benches that line the plaza."

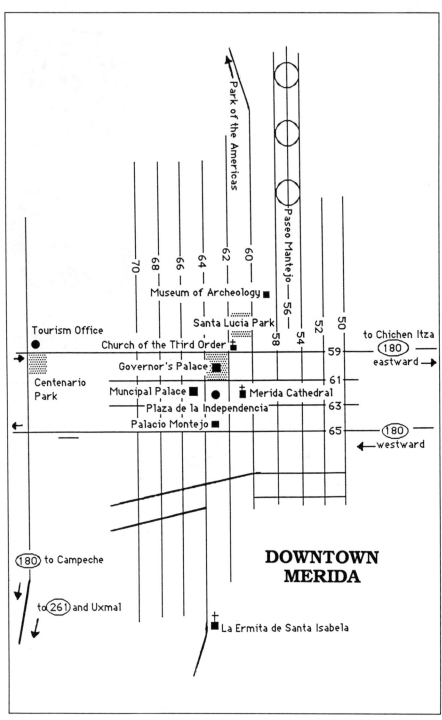

Park of the Americas

Paseo Mantejo — 56

70
68
66
64
62
60

Museum of Archeology ■

Santa Lucia Park

Tourism Office ●

52
50

Church of the Third Order ✝

to Chichen Itza

59

(180)

eastward →

Governor's Palace ■

Centenario
Park

Muncipal Palace ■   ●   ✝ Merida Cathedral

Plaza de la Independencia

61

Palacio Montejo ■

63

65

(180)

←westward

58
54

**DOWNTOWN
MERIDA**

(180) to Campeche

to (261) and Uxmal

✝
■ La Ermita de Santa Isabela

O nce there was a beautiful American journalist who came to Mexico by special invitation in recognition of an investigative series written in defense of the California Chicanos long years before that term came into vogue.

In the course of her travels, she caught the eye of the handsome governor of the war torn state of Yucatan. (Actually, it was more than his eye.) The governor wrote a love song for her. There were flowers, serenades, rides about the main square in a horse drawn calesa. He told her about the immense land reforms that he'd undertaken in an effort to give the Indians a share in the vast wealth that land owners were amassing at their expense. Obviously the two were made for each other.

He proposed; she accepted. The journalist was sailing to New York to buy her trousseau when she received word that her lover had been murdered by a cabal of land owners. She never married, choosing instead to devote the rest of her life to the fostering of Mexican culture.

The love song was *La Peregrina*. The governor was Felipe Carrillo Puerto, who was executed January 3, 1924. The journalist was Alma Reed who died in 1968. Alma's last wish was that she be buried beside Felipe and that's where she rests today.

The place was Merida.

Traces of a romantic past are very much a part of its lively present. Calesas still clop their way around the plaza and down the broad Paseo de Montejo. One can hear *La Peregrina* sung most any night. There's even a restaurant named for it.

The ghosts of Alma and Felipe walk the streets and others

do as well. You feel them at night when the white city turns to antique ivory in the lamplight. First there are the restless shades of the Mayas. The stone buildings of the 6th century ceremonial center of T'ho reminded the conquering Spaniards of the Roman ruins in Merida, Spain, so they leveled the Mayan stronghold and changed its name to Merida.

Francisco de Montejo had been trying for 15 years to conquer the inhabitants of the area. He celebrated his victory by "founding" Merida on January 6, 1542. The Mayan Indians were subsequently enslaved and put to work building the churches, mansions and government buildings with limestone snatched pre-cut from the ruins of their temples and palaces. Naturally one of the first residences constructed was Montejo's. Fifty-eight generations of the conquistador's descendants lived on in the grand mansion until it was sold to Banamex in 1980. Today you can cash your checks here—Banamex seems to give the best rates in town—while admiring the sweeping stairway, enormous courtyard and floors made of Carrara marble once brought from Italy as ballast by sea captains who returned home with the much prized *palo de tinte* or logwood. Outside you see the Montejo family crest, a foot planted firmly on the head of a Mayan slave, repeated the length of the building. One would hope the ghost of this arrogant conquistador would be an uneasy one.

As the hub of the giant "thumb" that comprises the Yucatan Peninsula, Merida was—until the advent of Cancun—the traditional gateway to the Maya country. It remains a principal tourist headquarters and hotel oasis. With a population of 450,000, Merida is the largest Mexican city east of Veracruz. With all of this, it has a very special flavor totally unlike any other city in Mexico. One could easily spend hours people watching while sitting on one of the lacy, wrought iron benches that line the plaza.

Isolated, insulated by geographical remoteness, a native considers himself a Yucateco first, a Mexican second. Nowhere is this individuality more apparent than in Merida. With no through highway from Mexico City until 1961 (and no railway until 1965), the Meridians frequently felt themselves more culturally linked to Europe than Mexico. It was easy for them to travel by ship to Spain, France, England, or Germany and easy for European colonists to reach them. Many young people were and are educated in Europe. When independence was finally won from Spain, Yucatecans were drawn to the total autonomy achieved by fellow Mayas in their newly established country of Guatemala. Permanent alliance with Mexico wasn't easily achieved. Yucatecos still consider themselves special and are. Quick, witty, independent, Meridians, in particular, look and act different from their not so near neighbors.

One obvious difference is their clothing. The *guayabera* , an open necked, handsomely pleated shirt, is worn everywhere. For women, the *huipil* has been the choice for centuries and still is often seen on the streets. This loose fitting white shift is richly embroidered in an opulent flower pattern at the square neckline and hemline and is worn over a lace trimmed petticoat. An accompaniment is the *rebozo de Santa Maria*, a stole of woven silk which can be tied in any number of attractive variations.

But clothing is only one small difference that distinguishes Meridians. The others become quickly apparent as the wonderful montage of diverse cultural influences comprising the city become apparent. Merida is an unusually easy city to explore because of the way the streets are numbered.

Even numbered *calles*, or streets, run north to south, odd numbered streets run east to west. All down town streets are one way. The main plaza, which remains the heart of town, is bordered by streets 60, 61, 62 and 63.

WHERE TO STAY

The, for the most part, narrow Meridian streets were constructed for calesas, not trucks, taxis, scooters, buses, etc. It can be noisy at night so, wherever you stay, try to book a hotel room as far from the street as possible.

Twenty years ago the Panamerican Hotel seemed the only choice. Today there are a plenitude of excellent hotels, but the *El Presidente Panamerican* still remains a charmer.
A snow white palace—one of the structures that helped to give Merida its title, "the white city,"–the hotel was once an elegant mansion.   Today one can luxuriate in old world opulence: white Corinthian columns,   marble nymphs around the central fountain, crystal chandeliers, high molded ceilings.   Upstairs in the new wing, the rooms are large, clean, simple. The food is good at the Panamerican. An excellent band plays for dancing and a colorful variety of Mayan folk dances are performed nightly. Though within easy walking distance of the old plaza where most activities center, the Panamerican is located in a quieter neighborhood.

Among the downtown hotels, the best bet–particularly well located for women traveling alone–is *Casa de Balam* on Calle 60. "The House of the Jaguar" is within a block of concerts, shops and excellent restaurants. After a day's shopping, the lush, tropical courtyard is a delightful oasis. The staff is pleasant and helpful, and there's an excellent travel agency in the building.

• • •
• • •

The *Montejo Palace* faces on the broad boulevard Paseo de Montejeo which some have likened to the Champs Elysees. It has a lively nightclub and a charming sidewalk cafe which spills out from the elegant veranda. From there it's fun to watch a passing scene that includes both old and new. One of the best offerings is the "sweet" man who strolls by balancing a tray on his head. My first day in town, I'd opted for a margarita and a seafood cocktail. But how could I resist that marvelous praline-like thing from amidst the beguiling assortment he offered? I couldn't. The maitre'd in passing remarked, "We have a saying, "One who takes a sweet with a drink is a very sweet drunk." We agreed that it probably lost something in translation. Anyway this is a friendly bastion.

For the budget minded, the elegant old *Gran Hotel* which faces on the Parque Cepeda is the best bet in town. A faded beauty with more than a touch of class, this former mansion has balcony views of the pretty park.

WHERE TO EAT

Portico del Peregrino, at 501 Calle 57, named for the song, is the kind of place that Alma and Felipe would have loved, a romantic restaurant with arched courtyards and delicious food.

But I think they would also have frequented *Pancho Villa's Follies,* at 509 Calle 59. The food is equally outstanding. (Lobster thermador practically for pennies.) The decor is Mayan funk, beaded lamps, a blaze of hot pink draperies, clashing happily with striped table cloths. How could you not love a place where the bandido waiters wear crossed cartridges and sombreros? These guys are friendly, funny, nice and that marvel in Mexico—fast. The music's lively, the ambience upbeat.   Wonderful photos of Pancho and his friends manage to look amusingly macho.

No one could ever call the waiters at *Ananda Maya Gynza Vegetarian Restaurant* at 507 Calle 59 fast or funny. Mexican waiters are almost invariably pokey by our standards, but this must be the place where the term laid back was born.   Since the restaurant *is* good, think of eating there as an opportunity to learn or practice meditation.   Or bring postcards to write or a book to read. If you don't happen to have a book with you, the situation can easily be remedied at the metaphysical bookstore conveniently located at the back of the restaurant. Sometimes there's live flamenco music , at other times an excellent tape.   The courtyard is pretty, an arched patio with a few pleasant but unpretentious shops.   The menu is a fanciful potpourri featuring possibilities like Tolkien onion rings or Kama Sutra croquettes.

There's nothing particularly romantic about *Soberanis* at 503 Calle 60 (facing the main plaza) The ambience is zero but the seafood's the tastiest in town and the prices are unbelievably cheap.   Just thinking about it makes me want to fly down for an oyster fix.

WHAT TO DO

The **Regional Museum of Archaeology** is a delight on several levels. As one of the finest provincial museums in Mexico, it brings into focus the history, culture and lifestyle of the Mayas. The building itself is an architectural gem, one of the most beautiful of the many mansions built along the Paseo Montejo by the henequen barons who became millionaires during the 19th and early 20th centuries when the sisal fields of Yucatan furnished the world with ropes and fibers . It's possible to see exhibits here that no longer exist at the sites themselves–displays of artifacts, reconstructed plans of old cities and an excellent explanation of how the people actually lived. Here in this opulent wedding cake of a mansion is an easy to digest overview of the ruins that exist in the area and beyond.

After exploring the museum, take a walk or a calesa ride up the **Paseo Montejo**. This eight-block, tree-lined thoroughfare with its extravagant monuments, mini-palaces and chalets patterned after a Parisian boulevard is one of the most amazing sights in Mexico.

Back in the center of town, the zocolo or **Plaza de la Independencia** is a perfect place to re-orient oneself. Prior to the conquest, the zocolo was the site of the great temple of H-Chum-caan, surrounded on all sides by other temples and pyramids. Today the only trace of them can be seen in the walls of the nearby cathedral.

Despite the busy world that borders it, the plaza retains its colonial charm. The S-shaped just-the-two-of-you stone love seats look like lacy valentines and above them the India laurel trees have a story of their own to tell. Two hundred years ago they were seedlings bound for Havana when a storm came up and sank the boat. Merida reaped the wild wind.

Facing the plaza on the east is the lemon colored cathedral begun in 1561. The building is massive–more massive than Merida merited in the eyes of the Spaniards, but by the time they discovered their mistake........It seems that the plans for a small cathedral originally slated for Merida were substituted accidentally for the more grandiose design meant for the cathedral in Lima. (Where the gold was.) Maybe this explains why the twin towers of Merida's

•••
•
=

cathedral are so dinky, seemingly out of scale with the rest of the building. This, perhaps, is where they realized the mistake.

Though the cathedral, finally finished in 1599, was built in the fortress style with wall slits to place firearms in case of an Indian attack, this feature didn't save it from being sacked during the 1917 revolution. A startling contrast to the churchly opulence seen in other parts of Mexico, this cathedral has a stark, stripped down look. It's one highlight sounds like the patron of footsore tourists–Christ of the Blisters. Actually the statue is reputed to be carved from a tree that burned all night without being destroyed. The statue was then placed in a church that caught fire. The next day the statue was found blistered but not burned and was transferred to the mother church in Merida.

The **Government Palace**, lined with murals by Yucatan's leading artist, Fernando Castro Pacheco, is a must-see. On the second floor is the hall of history filled with murals that depict the birth of the Mayas, their trials and tribulations, their gods, heroes, villains, the whole grand sweep of events on the Yucatan Peninsula from ancient times up until the 20th century. You can even see Felipe Carrillo Puerto, but not, unfortunately, Alma Reed.

The **Santa Lucia Square** on 60th Street, a block up from the Casa Balam, was once a stage stop for those arriving and departing the city. The 22 hooks where the horses were tied are still visible. Across the street is another poignant memory, a small stone chapel dappled and gray was built some 400 years ago for the use of the mulattoes and blacks brought to Yucatan as slaves by the Spanish conquistadores.

Happier memories are recreated on Thursday evenings

when the place comes alive again. An orchestra of guitars and brass begins to play. Women in *huipils* and men in white cotton suits appear before the floodlit wedding cake facade of white arches that partially enclose the square. They dance with trays of glasses balanced on their heads, they dance as matadors and bulls, they dance with woven ribbons around a maypole, they dance with baskets of fruit and colored shawls. It's very pretty and colorful; a wonderful place to catch the flavor of Meridian life as it was and still remains. Santa Lucia Square is also notable on Sundays as a flea market.

• SHOPPING

Merida's a good shopping town with opportunities literally everywhere. Many of the charming exhibits at the **Museum of Popular Art** are for sale. Another favorite haunt of mine is **Geboy's** on the corner of 60th and 57. This charming store has a wide variety of distinctive jewelry, smart and wearable variations of exotic clothing and unusual artifacts, well made and reasonably priced.

Both shoppers or none shoppers will be equally fascinated by the **Mercado Municipal,** a great, huge barnlike structure where everything from howler monkeys to gold jewelry can be obtained. You can find the pretty stoles called *rebozos de Santa Maria* here as well as *huipils* and richly embroidered blouses. You can also buy sandals, machetes, birds, birdcages, baskets, copal, gold encrusted bugs–anything you can imagine and more. If you like to bargain, this is certainly the place; but *do* inspect your treasures very carefully. What you buy may be slightly cheaper but often isn't as well made as the merchandise back in the high rent district. Whether you buy or not, the ambience of this place is not to be missed.

An arresting bas-relief at Mayapan

Mayapan
(my-ah-pahn)

"This was the last great Mayan stronghold and, for a time, the most important city in Yucatan. Today it's virtually forgotten."

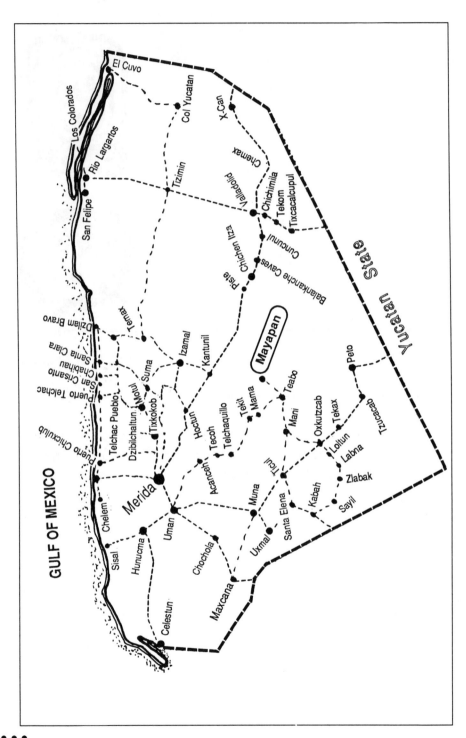

H unac Ceel was one of those take charge people who made his own luck. He was tired of the way things were going within the Triple Alliance, an organization of city states comprising Mayapan, Chichen Itza and Uxmal. As far as he was concerned, Chichen Itza was getting far too uppity; but as a commoner, there was nothing that he could do about it.

Well aware that under the strict cultural rules of the hierarchy he had no chance of ruling, Hunac Ceel decided to take both his own life and the destiny of his people into his hands. His big chance came when the authorities of Mayapan organized a pilgrimage to the sacred cenote at Chichen Itza. On this occasion many people were thrown into the well in the hope that at least one would return to the surface with a message from the gods concerning Mayapan's administration.

A collective sigh of disappointment arose from the crowd gathered about the rim of the well. The waters were ominously still, not one person had emerged from the depth. It was the moment for which Hunac Ceel—who'd secretly taught himself to swim—had been waiting. Suddenly he bounded forward and dove into the cenote.

The people gasped in astonishment as he disappeared into the blue-green waters and then cheered as he re-emerged. "I have spoken to the gods," Hunac Ceel cried out. The crowd was stunned into speechlessness when he revealed the full extent of the divine message. The gods had announced that he was to be king of the entire Yucatan peninsula.

Pulled from the well, Hunac Ceel was proclaimed Lord of Mayapan as well as all the cities of Yucatan. A man unwilling to leave anything to chance, he insured

Mayapan's supremacy by calling on Mexican mercenaries known as *ah canuls* or "protectors" to assist him. The *ah canuls* were expert archers credited with introducing the bow and arrow to Yucatan. The Cocom dynasty founded by the resourceful Hunac Ceel is believed to have lasted for 250 years.

Then in 1441 a gathering storm broke. The Mexican mercenaries were understandably unpopular from the beginning, and the Cocoms, as their patrons, were increasingly resented. The old angers smoldered until inevitably a boiling point was reached. Under the leadership of the Xius, the surrounding countryside rose up against Mayapan. The fortress city was destroyed, the Cocoms slaughtered with the exception of one son who was away.

The hated *Ah canuls* were driven from the area, some taking refuge in Tulum. After their victory over Mayapan, the Xius founded the city of Mani which means "it is past." Unfortunately this was just so much wishful thinking. Bygones refused to remain bygones. The surviving prince returned and founded the city of Tibulon which means "we are betrayed." The rest of Mayapan was split into a dozen or so small, angry communities. No one forgot anything.

This was the condition of things when the Spaniards arrived on the scene. Despite their lack of unity, the Mayas were able to repulse the invaders twice, literally pushing them from the land, but then the old enmity flared again. In 1536 the Xius undertook a pilgrimage to Chichen Itza and asked the Cocoms for safe conduct through their land. They were surprised by a warm welcome. For four days and nights the visitors were feted. It appeared that the old feuds were at last at an end.

It appeared wrong. The grandson of the slaughtered Mayapan king wasn't about to let this opportunity pass. The seeming hospitality was merely a ruse. On the fifth day the Cocoms fell on the unsuspecting Xius and massacred all of them.

This was the final nail in the coffin of unity. When the Spaniards returned for another try in 1540, they found a strife-torn land exhausted by civil war. The Maya could no longer resist the invaders with their superior arms and fearsome diseases. The country fell. In 1546 and again in 1547, the Mayas rose against the conquerors but by then it was too late.

The sense of loss, of devastation, is more apparent in Mayapan than any other site. This was the last great Mayan stronghold and, for a time, the most important city in Yucatan. Today it's virtually forgotten. Nineteen miles away in Merida, a bus leaves the main terminal every hour. It stops at Mayapan, but hardly anyone gets off. Too bad, the guide, obviously eager for company, is very helpful.

Wandering about the deserted ruins, one finds an ample base from which to speculate. The structures cover a vast area and have, for the most part, been left in their original state of decay. An air of lonely quiet pervades the site. Archaeological excavations serve only to emphasize Mayapan's architectural mediocrity, yet for well over two centuries this center dominated the entire Yucatan peninsula.

Unlike ruins in other areas of Yucatan, we *know* what happened in Mayapan. This was a city destroyed by war. In 1950, archaeologists found skeletons with flint spear points protruding from their bones. Today we can still detect burned beams and broken altars.

Unlike the other Mayan sites—primarily ceremonial centers—this was a real city. Its inhabitants were very like the ancient Romans, far more involved with military strength, empire building and administration than in esthetics or religion. Mayapan was a political city and a fortress. Very few of its buildings were temples, and those that existed were shabby, clumsy affairs, mute testimony to the cultural poverty of a military regime.

The ten thousand or so residents lived within walls, but in the end these barricades proved no protection. The tombs of the leaders tell a grisly story of massacres that must have taken place in the midst of funeral rites. In one tomb, 41 skeletons surround one skeleton, who appears to have been their master in life.

Here was a government primarily occupied with power and war. Its obsession ultimately resulted in oblivion.

The crumbling ruins of Mayapan

Xlacah cenote is a fine swimming hole

Dzibilchaltun
(see-bee-eel-chahlt-toon)

" Hundreds of structures have been uncovered in this major metropolis and archaeologists estimate that there may be at least 8000 more. Its size and the fact that it wasn't periodically deserted as were most of the other cities, have lead to speculation that Dzibilchaltun may have literally been the capital of Mayadom."

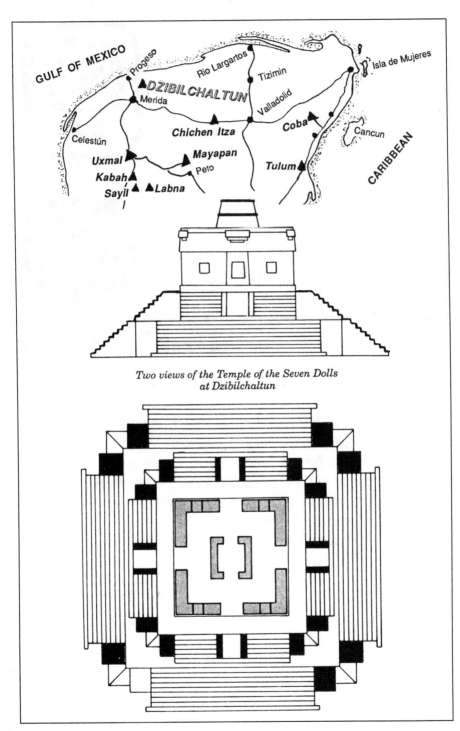

Two views of the Temple of the Seven Dolls
at Dzibilchaltun

T he tree-ringed cenote, a limestone sinkhole at the ancient city of Dzibilchaltun, holds secrets of the past.

It also holds potential pleasure for the present. Pilgrims to this seemingly forgotten—yet easily accessible—Mayan stronghold should bring their bathing suits.

Dzibilchaltun, "the place where there are symbols inscribed on flat stones," is the oldest Mayan city continuously in use. This vast site—dating from 2000 B.C. until after the Spanish conquest—is spread over an estimated 25 square miles. Hundreds of structures have been uncovered in this major metropolis and archaeologists estimate that there may be at least 8000 more. Its size and the fact that it wasn't periodically deserted as were most of the other cities, have lead to speculation that Dzibilchaltun may have literally been the capital of Mayadom.

Despite all this, Dzibilchaltun is a kind of stepchild. First, of course, there were the Spaniards. The conquistadores razed many of the structures to build the inevitable church. You can see this edifice as you approach the site. It stands out immediately because of the very broad arch. (The Mayas utilized only the narrow Korbel, or "false" arch.) Today that monument to arrogance and bigotry is merely another ruin.

Unfortunately the plundering didn't end there. Over the years local builders continued the tradition, blithely destroying temples whenever they needed building materials. Archaeological digs sponsored by Tulane University and the National Geographic Society begun in the 1950s may have put an end to the devastation, but Dzibilchaltun is still virtually ignored, a place somehow lost in time.

Located just off the Progresso Road, the site is easy to reach by bus or car. There's a small museum just outside the ruins and a minimal entrance fee. Usually you can have this extensive site to yourself. It's a wonderful place to spend the day wandering at will, picnicking and swimming.

Xlacah, the sacred cenote, makes a delicious swimming hole. Bathing's permitted, the water's sparkling clear, water lilies grow toward the shallow end, the deep end descends to 55 meters at least 100 feet farther than the better known well at Chichen Itza. Some of the bones and other artifacts found here are on display at the museum.

The **Temple of the Seven Dolls,** reached at the end of a 500-yard *sacbe* leading from the large central area, seems small and unimposing from a distance but has been beautifully restored. It's unusual because of its square plan, two windows in the sides of the main structure– Mayan builders apparently didn't do windows!– and the pyramid form in the roof comb. All of these are considered unique in Mayan architecture. The temple has been carbon dated as a fifth century structure which places it in the Classic period. Each of the seven terra cotta figures found inside portray a different physical defect. Were they a kind of voodoo doll? Or possibly a healing tool? Ponder their use in the museum as you leave.

••••
•

Temple of the Magician – Uxmal

Uxmal
(oosh-mall)

"The city of Uxmal (600-l000 AD) is a stunning example of Classic Mayan architecture, visually the most dramatic site in the Puuc "highlands" and, some believe, in all of Yucatan. Grouped as they are on a broad plateau, the buildings appear almost unreal. "

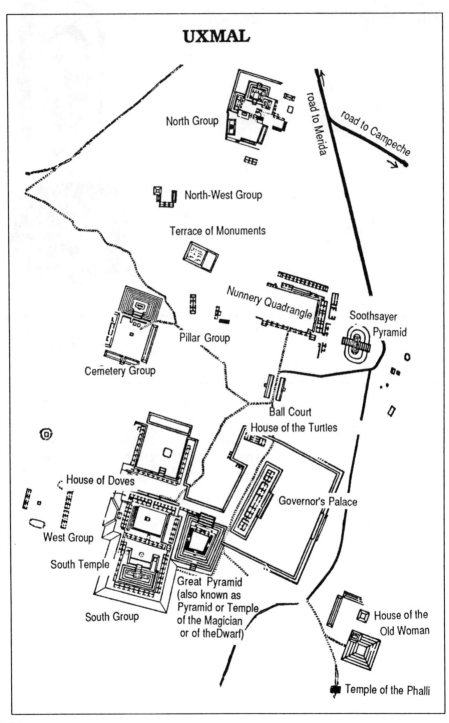

UXMAL

North Group

road to Merida

road to Campeche

North-West Group

Terrace of Monuments

Nunnery Quadrangle

Soothsayer Pyramid

Pillar Group

Cemetery Group

Ball Court

House of the Turtles

House of Doves

Governor's Palace

West Group

South Temple

Great Pyramid
(also known as
Pyramid or Temple
of the Magician
or of theDwarf)

South Group

House of the
Old Woman

Temple of the Phalli

T hat the architecture of Uxmal should be frequently likened to the Acropolis seems appropriate for a ghost town haunted by parallels to both Hercules and Helen of Troy.

According to legend, Uxmal was founded by a dwarf. Obviously the dwarf lacked the physical attributes of the Greek super hero, but he was more than Hercules's equal in luck, cunning and chutzpah. Both were assigned seemingly impossible tasks, both succeeded and received rich rewards achieving a kind of demi-god status.

The story of the miraculous dwarf begins with the kind of prophecy we've heard many times. A king is warned that his kingdom must be forfeited when a magic cymbal is struck by a man not born of woman. The improbability of it all insures the king's complacency.

In this story the king's domain was a small, insignificant one, his palace only a white house; but his was the only game in town and he liked it that way. Naturally it was all too good to last.

In a tiny hut on the edge of town lived an old woman skilled in sorcery, a woman with strange friends in mysterious places. Some rightly called her a witch for she did many marvelous things like concoct midnight potions that could both cause and cure illness. (It's said that the ancestors of the present day *curanderos,* or witch doctors, learned their skills from her.)

One morning the woman woke feeling *old* . What I need to cheer me is a child, she decided. That night the witch went to the dark caves in the hills where the hunchbacked ones live. There one of her colleagues gave her a great egg. The witch brought the egg home and secretly buried it in the

• • • •

•
=

earth to hatch. A few days later out popped a boy with the face of a man. To avoid embarrassment (a baby at her age!), the old woman introduced him as her grandson.

The child was unusually precocious—he could talk from birth—but his physical growth stopped when he was only 7 hands high. The bright boy was aware almost from the beginning that his grandmother was no ordinary lady. Soon he was snooping about the hut trying to learn her secrets. The dwarf was certain that there was something buried under the hearth. Finally this bratty kid tricked the witch by puncturing her water jar so that she would remain at the well a long, long time.

During her absence, he dug into the ashes and pulled out a golden cymbal and a little rod. Of course the dwarf struck the cymbal, but even he was surprised by the results. The sound was like thunder, the earth trembled, and there was a great uproar as people ran out of their houses.

The king heard the mighty roar and shuddered. The words of the forgotten prophecy came back to him: The mighty city of Uxmal will appear in the place that bears that name. Whatever man may be seated on the throne let him prepare to leave it for no one can resist the king who is coming.

The incumbent had no intention of bowing to the inevitable. He ordered his warriors to find the person who'd struck the cymbal and to bring him back. When they returned with the tiny dwarf everyone laughed and the king breathed a sigh of relief.

"So you're the one who would be king," he greeted the boy. "That's all very well, but first you must prove yourself. There are three tests. To begin with you must prove that you have more wisdom than I. Tell me without omitting a single berry how many fruits hang in the branches of the sacred ceiba tree?"

Without blinking an eye, the young dwarf replied: "One hundred thousand twice 60 and 3 times 3 and if you don't believe me, count them one by one."

As the king looked at the tree uncertain of what to do next, a great bat swooped down and whispered in his ear: "The boy spoke the truth."

The king turned pale and bowed his head, but raised it again. Power was sweet and not to be relinquished easily. "Tonight let us each make a statue in our own image and tomorrow we shall compare which is the most beautiful and durable."

The boy agreed . That night he constructed not only a statue but–with the help of his witch patron and her hunchback friends–a broad white *sacbe* . The next day he and the witch returned to town on it. Behind them followed a procession of townspeople who no longer considered the dwarf a laughing matter.

The king's statue was attractive enough but made of wood. When put to a test, it burned; but the dwarf's statue was made of wet clay and the fire baked it fine and hard.

People began to crowd about the dwarf congratulating him, their allegiance clearly shifting. There'll be one more test," the king insisted.

"I shall command a scaffold to be built tonight," he told the boy. "Tomorrow the executioner shall break open thy head with a mallet of steel. If you can survive that, you will be king."

Once more the boy agreed, but added, "If I come out alive will you submit to the same test?" And the king who should have known better said, "Yes."

"Spend the night here with me in my house," he then suggested to the contender. The boy refused. The king's little white house was simply not up to his standards of what a palace should be, so overnight the dwarf and his magical helpers constructed a new one.

The following morning the crafty kid went smiling to the scaffold. He was still smiling when he knelt before the executioner and even when he rose again—the witch had hidden a copper plate under his hair which deflected the mallet blow. Now it was the king's turn and he did not survive the test.

On the next night the small village was transformed into the great city of Uxmal —temples, palaces, courtyards.   It's the same magnificent city that we see today with the Temple of the Dwarf (more frequently called the Temple of the Magician) dominating the scene.

Uxmal thrived for hundreds of years and part of its success was due to a triple alliance with Chichen Itza and Mayapan which the canny dwarf-magician was said to have founded.   The Triple Alliance was all well and good until it turned into a triangle......and that's another story.

Princess Sac-Nicte was beautiful.   Canek, the young king of Chichen Itza, was handsome. When they met by chance it was love at first sight. Unfortunately there was one major drawback, the lovely daughter of Hunac Ceel, the Lord of Mayapan, was engaged to the King of Uxmal.

Perhaps Sac-Nicte pleaded with her father. But her romantic preferences were of little importance to him. As the daughter of a king, hers was a marriage of state. The agreement had been made, a slight to the King of Uxmal unthinkable. The wedding plans continued.

At last the day came when Hunac Ceel brought his daughter to Uxmal for the nuptial ceremony. People bearing lavish gifts flocked to the great city from all corners of the Triple Alliance. Then a murmur arose. Where was King Canek's tribute? Where, for that matter, was King Canek? Could such a strange behavior go ignored?

The three day marriage ceremony began, one day of festivities, then a second day. Princess Sac-Nicte walked through the rituals as though in a trance. Then on the third day King Canek arrived with a large army and literally swept her off her feet. In the confusion, the lovers disappeared leaving the three armies of Uxmal, Mayapan and Chichen Itza to slug it out among themselves.

While Sac-Nicte and Canek were settling into married life in Peten—their chosen lovenest—the forces of Chichen Itza were devastated by the combined armies of Mayapan and Uxmal. The survivors are then said to have abandoned Chichen Itza, scattering into fragments which would one day rally to overthrow the descendants of Hunac Ceel and his hated mercenaries.

These legends make as much sense as what we actually know about Uxmal, for it, too, was ultimately abandoned. To leave such a place would be tantamount to walking away from the Empire State Building or the Transamerica Pyramid in San Francisco. Yet we know Uxmal was abandoned. Why?

We know it was rebuilt as many as five times. Why again? Why was it built even once? There is almost no water in the area. Yucatan is one vast limestone slab with rivers running underground. In some places the rock has caved in, forming great natural wells of water which are called cenotes. These are prominent at other ruins, but there are none at Uxmal. Here the Mayan builders carved giant reservoirs, but surely there were years when there was no rain. It's easy to understand the prevalence of Chac, the elephant nosed rain god, on so many of the buildings.

WHAT TO SEE

The city of Uxmal (600-1000 AD) is a stunning example of Classic Mayan architecture, visually the most dramatic site in the Puuc "highlands" and, some believe, in all of Yucatan. Grouped as they are on a broad plateau, the buildings appear almost unreal.

These exquisitely proportioned structures extend over an area of about one-half mile in length and 600 yards in width. The site comprises seven known architectural groupings, three of which have been partially restored. Each of these has been placed in a highly precise fashion: The **Pyramid of the Magician** (sometimes called Pyramid of the Dwarf) in a vertical line, the **Quadrangle of the Nunnery** in a square and the **Governor's Palace** in a horizontal line.

The sound and light show dramatically highlights the intricate geometric patterns for which Uxmal is famous; but under any lighting conditions, this place is a marvel. A marvel? Miracle is more like it. There were no mines on the Yucatan peninsula, no metal tools used in construction, no dray animals and the wheel as a means of conveyance was unknown. Are the dwarf's fabled feats any more amazing than this?

The **Temple of the Magician** clearly dominates the site, stirring the imagination despite the forbidding, unapproachable aspect it presents from every angle. A flight of 118 steps leads to its two platforms. (A chain was added in 1865 to facilitate the Empress Carlota's climb and many are grateful for it today.) The pyramid is actually five superimposed temples, each embedded in the other—a synthesis in stone of centuries of continual occupation. Each of the succeeding sanctuaries buried the proceeding one, thereby altering its orientation.

Temple One, almost at ground level, was buried in rubble when the pyramid itself was built. Once it was uncovered, a fine facade was revealed decorated with Chac masks, astronomical symbols and human figures. Access to Temple Two, the walls of which were painted in a serpent motif, was by a stairway on the east side. Temple Three, embedded within the pyramid, is invisible from the outside. One enters Temple Four through the stone jaws of the rain god Chac—a grim reminder of a sacred rite passage. According to Mayan tradition, one must die in the jaws of the god in order to be reborn into a new life which followed initiation.

From Temple Five which is spread out over the summit of the pyramid, one has a plumed serpent's view of the entire site. For instance, the small ruined pyramid directly to the south is the **Pyramid of the Old Woman,** believed to be the former home of the dwarf's grandmother who didn't die at all and is believed to be alive and well and living with a pet snake at the bottom of a well somewhere not far away.

The biggest building is the **Governor's Palace.** If it looks that grand, it must have been the governor's palace–or so the Spaniards thought when they observed the abandoned structure 500 years after its abandonment.   Today we know that this is the place where Mayan astronomer-priests once took measurements and consulted planetary charts as they watched Venus rise at dawn. Their calculations linked planting, harvesting and celebrating with propitious astronomical events.   One of the most awe inspiring of the latter occurred every eight years when the planet Venus rose on the horizon at a point aligned with with the center door of the palace.

Governor's Palace – Uxmal

The 318-foot long structure rests on three vast terraces overlooking the city. The effect is massive, grand, a little heartless. It's been called the most spectacular building in Pre-Columbian America and is frequently favorably compared with Greek architecture. The palace is made up of a central edifice and two side structures. It's main facade contains 11 entrances with vaulted passageways and lateral wings.

The stone frieze above it resembles nothing more than a bolt of shear lace. This exquisite construction is ten feet tall and surrounds the entire palace. The 2,200 square feet of surface bears mute testimony to the innumerable technical difficulties faced and surmounted by its creators. The theme of the cross vault, making up the motif of the frieze is composed of 20,000 identical carved stones, each weighing several pounds.   In addition to this there are also 150 Chac masks three feet long and almost two feet high, numerous stylized serpents and altogether more than 20,000 different carved stones placed tightly together. How did they do it?

Near the entrance to the site is the beautiful **Quadrangle of the Nunnery**. First let me tell you that no nuns ever lived there. It wasn't a pleasure palace where vestals enjoyed the wild life prior to their sacrifice to Chac either. Very probably the "nunnery" was once a kind of elitist boarding school. Its architecture is distinguished by edifices at the four cardinal points each of which opens onto the center courtyard.

The northern edifice with its 13 double rooms may have been reserved for the most prestigious of the young lords. It's the largest and most important structure in the quadrangle and is flanked by two diminutive temples, one being the Temple of Venus. Some of the lintels are original and the top of the door wall is a false front of intricately carved huts and Chacs.

The eastern edifice is the simplest and the best preserved. Here the lattice pattern flares elegantly upward toward the top of the building where the head of an owl—the omen of death—is inserted.

In the western edifice the ornamental motif is an imposing throne bearing a figure with the head of an old man and the body of a turtle. On the frieze, two plumed serpents reach out toward the corners of the facade with a human head in their open jaws. Other parts of the stone sculpture depicts men with tattooed genitals.

The southern edifice in the quadrangle has eight rooms. Above the door of each is a stone sculpture of a *na* or Maya cottage looking exactly as they look today but for the inevitable Chac mask on the roof. On the ceiling arc red handprints similar to the one at Tulum.

Is there a link between the **House of the Turtles** and the stone figure of the man who's half man and half turtle in the quadrangle? The house, located "next door," gets its name from a row of turtles crawling across the facade. The understated elegance, economy of line and balanced proportions of this building call to mind a classic Greek temple.

There are other ruins to explore: the pretty **House of the Doves** which is laid out in a manner similar to the Quadrangle and gets its name from its undulating roof combs; the **Ball Court**, a small affair thought to be a kind of training camp for Chichen Itza Olympics; the **Cemetery Group** and the **Western Group,** both as yet barely touched by archaeologists.

Phalli are very big in Uxmal. I just had to say it! The Empress Carlota was so impressed she wrote home about it. There's very little eroticism in Mayan art or architecture. Uxmal is an exception. Ornamenting the building ironically called the "Nunnery," is a frieze of naked men and the Governor's Palace contains a phallus of proportions stupendous enough to embarrass some visitors while amusing others.

Following an obscure little path on a dutiful pilgrimage to the **House of the Old Woman**–unfortunately this shrine to the woman who started it all is in shambles–I passed a sacred grove of stone known as the **Phallus Collection.** Some are erect, others fallen, a kind of petrified forest of fertility.   And that's really what it's all about. Fertility was all important in this drought-ridden agricultural area.

Nearby is the **Temple of the Phalli**, named for its unusual representations of this symbol.   They were even used as water spouts to drain water.   One can imagine their effect during the rainy season.

Which brings me back to that all important subject of rain. The mask of Chac is everywhere in Uxmal. It reaches out from friezes, fills in corners, and clings to the spaces above doorways.   The Chac features–the sneering, half-open mouth exposing jutting fangs, the horns, globular eyes and snout like nose–were designed to be awesome.   And they are.

They also bear a striking similarity to the Chinese *t'oa t'ie* mask of the Chang period. How tempting to search for some form of relationship between them despite the geographic separation and a time gap of some 2000 years.

Nearly 1000 years has passed since Uxmal was abandoned but Chac remains very much alive. In a land of little rain, he continues to control the agricultural destiny of the Mayas. Despite the, at times, forcible efforts of the clergy to destroy him, Chac is a god who will not die, a deity still venerated in secret ceremonies.

GETTING THERE & WHERE TO STAY _____

The breathtaking ruins of Uxmal are located in the Puuc (pook) hills 50 miles south of Merida on Highway 261. Any number of tours will take you there or you can easily travel the distance by car or bus. There are five buses a day which leave the main bus station in Merida, the price less than $1.

One night and two days at Uxmal are a must, but two nights and three days would be still better. This is a fascinating site surrounded by other attractions.

The closest hotel to the ruins is the ***Villa Arqueologica,*** another in the Club Med run chain. If you're looking for typical Club Med "action," you won't find it here–the bar closes at 10; but, as at the other hotels in the chain, the ambience is attractive, the food and amenities adequate.

Hacienda Uxmal remains my favorite. It has something to do with vibes.   The place was originally built as a headquarters for the archaeologist excavating Uxmal more than fifty years ago and has been well maintained.   Many of the large, airy rooms with their blocky 1930s furniture and ceiling fans are built around an expansive courtyard, an Edenlike abstraction from the surrounding jungle.

A pleasant choice for the budget minded is **Hotel Mision Uxmal**, a bit farther from the ruins, but not too far. This one, too, has a pool and restaurant.

Uxmal may be a bit short on nightlife–the one attraction is the slightly inane, but still spectacular sound and light show–unless you count, as I do, the appeal of spending the night in a Mayan ghost town.   Anyway, the day time potential is dazzling.

The petrified forest – Uxmal

The Arch of Labna

The Puuc Hill Country
(pook)

*" . . . the road unrolls like a ribbon offering a comparatively effortless opportunity to experience a whole new dimension of Mayan life and architecture. Like Uxmal, the cities of **Kabah, El Sayil, Labna** and **Zlapak** belong to the late Classic period and feature such Puuc elements as decorative clusters of columns and hallways of columns which once supported temple roofs."*

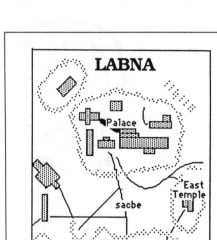

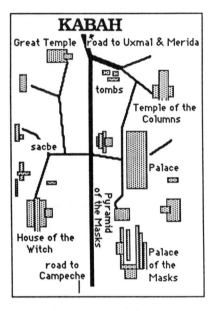

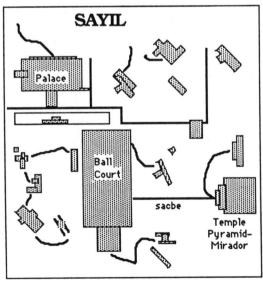

Twenty years ago I set off into the Puuc hinterlands with a jeep and driver. To me, it was a grand adventure. The driver was a Poncho Villa clone who packed a rifle and a machete. The machete came in very handy for the road was an overgrown track and the driver stopped many times to hack our way through the seemingly impenetrable walls of dense, brushy woodland.

Later as we shared a picnic lunch outside the temple at Zlapak, I tried to convey some of the excitement I felt. He grimaced, for him it was a hard way to make a living. A few weeks before he'd taken a party of anthropologists out to the site. As they'd climbed into the jeep for the return trip, a woman newly arrived to the area spoke up. "Okay, you've shown us how rough it can be, you've given us the jungle tour. Now take us back on the *real* road."

The wonder was still apparent in his eyes as he recalled the incident. After a weary sigh of resignation, he asked. "Do you imagine that I'd work so hard if there was any other way?"

It wasn't until 1978 that a real road was constructed linking this "new" network of Mayan cities with their big sister Uxmal. Today the road unrolls like a ribbon offering a comparatively effortless opportunity to experience a whole new dimension of Mayan life and architecture. Like Uxmal, the cities of **Kabah, Sayil, Labna** and **Zlapak** belong to the late Classic period and feature such Puuc elements as decorative clusters of columns and hallways of columns which once supported temple roofs.

Puuc, incidentally, refers to the late Classic period and to the slightly hilly country where this style of architecture flourished. These hill towns are still out of the way enough not to be crowded with tourists. They're intimate, less intimidating than Uxmal.

The surrounding jungle, though not of the "Tarzan" variety with tall trees blotting out the sun, has undergrowth so dense that it actually chokes out trees before they can grow tall.   Trails lead past mounds of overgrown rubble, the remains of one-time Mayan dwellings and temples where fallen idols wear spring bonnets of orchids. Climb to the top of one of these mysterious mounds and a vast chunk of southern Yucatan is yours for the viewing.

KABAH–Located 19 miles south of Uxmal–straddles Highway 261. The name, "He with a strong hand," is derived from a monumental stone figure of a naked man with a serpent in his hand which was found among the ruins. As is usually the case, the name was applied to the site long after the inhabitants had vanished.

Perhaps settlement here was an impressive experiment, one that proved useless in the long run. The ubiquitous Chac masks bear witness to the fervent prayers that were offered up to the rain god. The magnificent facade of the *Codz-Pop*, or **Temple of the Masks,** decorated as it is by row upon row of identical masks–250 of them–set so close together that there's hardly a gap between them seems to represent a colossal effort to bring the forces of nature under control.

This amazing structure which dominates the large temple complex on the east side of the site may have been placed there in gratitude. Before the temple is something more precious than gold or jewels– an ancient well still filled with life-giving water. This treasure was unique in Puuc country. Other settlements had to depend on *choltunes,* or man-made cisterns with their often inadequate supply of rainwater.

Where Uxmal exemplifies the essential simplicity and

uncluttered lines of the Puuc style, some of the Chenes look
of Chichen Itza seems apparent in the rich facade of the
Codz-Pop; but, Chenes or Puuc, there's simply nothing
like this anywhere in Mayadom.

Parts of the building, which once consisted of ten large
rooms, have fallen away to betray the builder's technical
secrets. The structure of the Korbel or "false "arch is laid
bare here. For all their architectural achievements, the
Mayas never discovered the principle of the true arch made
with a keystone and many smaller fitted stones. Instead,
they improvised with the Korbel arch which consisted of a
systematic placement in which each stone was cut longer
than the one below it, so that a heavier weight above would
press down and hold the lower stone in place. The longer
stones, arching toward each other, formed a kind of vault.

Once you've seen *Codz-Pop* which means in Mayan "rolled
mat" or "Lord of the Mat" possibly for Chac's elephant
snout, you've seen the highlight of Kabah, but there are still
other things to explore. Close by the Temple of the Masks
an overgrown path leads off into the jungle to more partially
restored buildings and mounds covering temples waiting to
be "discovered." A walk along this path will give you a
sense of the way it used to be and the way it could be again—
any time the highway department stopped cutting back the
intrusive growth which creeps back almost before your
eyes.

Another **Kabah** attraction is located across the highway.
It's an impressive arch which once marked the beginning
of a *sacbe* extending all the way to Uxmal. The 19th century
explorer, John Stephens likened it to a triumphant Roman
arch. What legions marched this way and when?

SAYIL–(Continue south 3 miles on Highway 261 to the new side road, Highway 184, **Sayil** is less than 3 miles further)– Partially restored, the 100-room **Palace** presents a completely new aspect of Mayan architecture which reminds everyone of something different. Some say a Greek temple, others a Renaissance palazzo, still others a Babylonian ziggurat. To me, it has a distinctly Minoan feeling until I confront the extended Chac masks at corners of the frieze. Inside we meet an old friend, the Descending God-Spaceman whose likeness was first encountered hundreds of miles away in Tulum.

Palace at Sayil

Off in the jungle behind the **Palace** is **El Mirador**, "the lookout." This pretty temple with its vaulted ceiling and slotted roofcomb is situated on the highest point of the highest pyramid.

Beyond **El Mirador** is a stela bearing a phallic figure of monumental proportions. The guides keep telling me that the Mayas didn't go in for this sort of thing. Perhaps it's unique in more ways than one.

ZLAPAK (Shlah-pawk)–3 miles down the road–the name means "old walls" and they are. Despite the new road, this tumble down temple doesn't seem to have changed a bit since I saw it twenty years ago–or probably John Stephens' visit in the early 1840s.

Once again one sees tier upon tier of masks, collonettes and Chac noses. Nearby is the old jeep track, almost overgrown but still offering access to abundant bird and bug life and an opportunity to explore further.

LABNA–3 miles farther down 184–is believed to be the architectural prototype of Uxmal. The lavishly ornamented **Arch of Labna**, a far grander structure than the better known Kabah arch, was once a passageway leading to a courtyard surrounded–as in Uxmal's Nunnery Quadrangle–by edifices that no longer exist. This is the largest and most ornate archway known to have been built by the Mayas.

Others **Labna** structures include **El Mirador**, another "lookout" on top of a pyramid. This one has rounded corners at its base similar to those at the Temple of the Magician. A closer look at this pretty, airy building reveals a macabre touch–a row of death heads carved into the roofcomb

The **Palace** is distinguished by a *chaltune* built into its second story. Thus far, 60 *chaltunes* have been located here indicating that this abandoned site once had a sizable population.

LOLTUN–A little over 18 miles past Labna on the way to Oxkutzcab (that's ohsh-kootz-kahb) are the **Loltun** caves, the largest known network of caverns on the Yucatan Peninsula.

A visit to **Loltun**, which means "stone flower," is a kind of time trip. Each step of the ascent is a shift backward toward a primordial past. Along the way there are artifacts such as *choltunes* placed strategically about for catching rain water and *metates* or corn grinders.

Myriad formations of stalactites and stalagmites bear striking resemblance to any number of things from the Virgin of Guadalupe to a phallus. One cavern is a Hugh Hefner extravaganza comprised of thousands of mammaries. Searching for all the possibilities adds to the "guided fantasy" feeling about this excursion.

When tapped, giant floor to ceiling columns give out a resonant hum: "Loll-tuuuuuuuuuun." There are carvings in the natural stone walls and handprints thought to date from 2000 BC are outlined in black. A complete set of mastodon bones has been discovered here and a large stone head. There's also a cave with two ladders, one leading out of the cave complex and another leading to a ledge with a small doorway leading to a ritual chamber.

These caves have twice sheltered the Mayas; first in ancient times and later as a fortress and refuge during the War of the Castes. Its intriguing to speculate about the lives of these cave dwellers while walking through what must have been their very living rooms; but the most exciting aspect of the tour is yet to come.

There *is* light at the end of the tunnel! Finally the passageway emerges into a two-story high cavern open to the sky at the top. Ancient, towering trees thrust their way up through the sunny opening and dust-flecked shafts of sunbeams light up the black recesses of the cave. Leafy green vines twine their way down into the immense chamber from above, often wrapping themselves about the exposed roots of the trees. The sense of having emerged from a time capsule into a prehistoric era is a mystical experience not soon to be forgotten.

But there's more, yet another puzzle to ponder. Two American researchers, anthropologist Michael d' Obrenovic and archeologist Manson Valentine, decided to explore the vast uncharted areas of the cave system. Both had an unexplainable sense of danger. D'Obrenovic took photographs. Despite his previous success in photographing caves, only one out of nine shots turned out. The ninth picture revealed a swirling mass of glowing energy that illuminated the entire passage.

D'Obrenovic had no explanation for the phenomenon "unless the old legends are true and we somehow succeeded in photographing an energy force left by the old priests to guard the sacred area." Scientists endeavoring to X-ray the Great Pyramid of Egypt enountered this same mysterious force field.

Loltun

The jungle encroaches on Palenque

Palenque
(pa-len-kay)

" Only partially redeemed from the jungle, Palenque remains a magnificent sight which rivals the sanctuary of Apollo at Delphi. Gleaming like alabaster, it lies upon the dark flanks of the Tumbala Mountains in the midst of a rain forest."

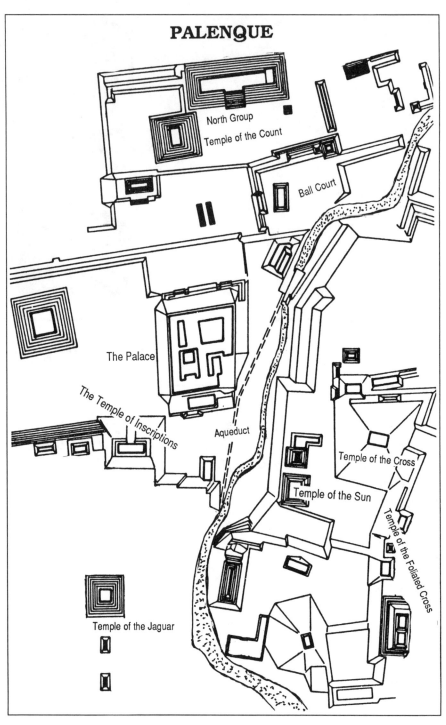

PALENQUE

North Group

Temple of the Count

Ball Court

The Palace

The Temple of Inscriptions

Aqueduct

Temple of the Cross

Temple of the Sun

Temple of the Foliated Cross

Temple of the Jaguar

I n 1773 a bored priest heard a wild story that made his day.

A passing Indian told of an abandoned city deep in the jungle—a city far different, grander, more beautiful than anything he'd ever seen or heard about. The city, he explained, was located in the jungle near the village of Santo Domingo del Palenque.

Father Ramon de Ordonez y Aguilar, canon of Cuidad Real (now San Cristobal de las Casas), could scarcely believe the tale. A little more than 200 years before the great Cortes himself must have marched right by the place and somehow missed it. Impossible as it all sounded, the idea of being the official discoverer of such a relic was titillating. He decided to mount an expedition to discover the truth for himself.

Father Ordonez's dutiful parishioners carried him the sixty miles to Santo Domingo del Palenque in a sedan chair. Presumably after a brief rest, they picked him back up and hiked another eight miles into the dense jungle.

The sight that awaited was stunning. Here was the most beautiful Mayan city of all, each building a work of art, intricately carved stone with the elegance of marble against a backdrop of emerald green.

As Father Ordonez studied the ruins—surely the most lovely in all of Mexico, if not the world—he recalled a legend about a charismatic leader named Votan who'd come to the area many hundreds of years before from across the Atlantic Ocean. The story was said to have been recorded by Votan himself in the Quiche dialect which the mysterious stranger had learned. The chronicle told of how he had come with his followers, introducing ideas and customs to the natives who offered their daughters in marriage. Ordonez's predecessor had burned this remarkable manuscript along with everything else pagan in an *auto de fe* very like that of Bishop de Landa. Fortunately a few sections had been copied for the select eyes of those deemed devout enough to read without fear of corruption. Ordonez had been one of these.

Puzzling over the account that had so fascinated him in his youth, Ordonez remembered that Votan had written of a sea journey from his far away homeland, Chivim, via the "Dwelling of the Thirteen". After reaching the Yucatan Peninsula, he'd journeyed up the Usumacinta River and founded a great city.

This must have been the city, Ordonez decided, surveying the magnificent ruins before him. He later theorized that Chivim was Tripoli in Phoenicia and the "Dwelling of Thirteen" must have been the Canary Islands. Since Votan's symbol was the snake, Ordonez named his find the "Great City of Serpents." Mayan archaeology began with his preliminary investigation.

Ordonez's story piqued the curiosity of King Charles III of Spain who, in 1787, ordered a systematic exploration of the ruins.   The assignment fell to an unlikely candidate.   Don Antonio del Rio, later recalled as "wafting through the jungles of Palenque an aroma of the latest fashionable scent," was a true dandy refusing to forsake his three cornered hat and powdered wig.

Despite his dress sense, Del Rio was a man of action. Maybe too much action. He very quickly hired 200 Indians who hacked away at the ruins with their axes and ma-chetes. As his proud reports states, "By dint of perseverance I effected all that was necessary to be done so that ultimately there remained neither a window nor a doorway blocked up; a partition that was not thrown down, nor a room, a corridor, court, tower, nor subterranean passage in which excavations were not effected from two or three yards in depth." Imagine the reaction of today's painstaking archaeologist.

Del Rio's account, which found its way into print 25 years later, was the first published book on Mayan archaeology. He concluded that the ruins at Palenque were probably made by early Roman colonizers, but didn't rule out a Phoenician connection.

The next adventurer to appear on the scene was by far and away the most colorful. Jean-Frederic, Count de Waldeck, had been the student of artist Jacques Louis David, the friend of Lord Byron, Beau Brummel and Marie Antoinette (whom he'd visited in prison shortly before her execution), had campaigned with Napoleon in Egypt, then become a pirate preying on British shipping in the Indian Ocean.

Now at a time when others might have looked forward to a quiet, comfortable retirement, de Waldeck determined to explore and sketch the ruins of Palenque. Many would have thought sixty-four a bit old for a jungle expedition into an area of hostile natives and incredibly difficult terrain but surely not de Waldeck who would–in his nineties–turn down a handsome cash settlement in favor of an anuity.

Reaching Palenque at last, de Waldeck selected the prettiest ruin and the most nubile of the village ladies and set up housekeeping. (The ruin is still referred to as the "Count's Temple.") From this vantage point he produced ninety extraordinary drawings

But for all his talent and enterprise, the Count was not an

untypical tourist. John Stephens, the next adventurer on the scene, happened upon de Waldeck's name scribbled on the wall of the Palace beside the drawing of a woman, (probably the mestizo mistress) with the date 1832. De Waldeck's drawings were incorporated into a book in which he concluded that the Chaldeans and Hindus were responsible for the construction of Palenque. The book was eventually published in 1866 when the incomparable count was 100 years old.

So many theories, so much conjecture, this much is known today: Palenque, uninhabited since the ninth century, but still pulsating with a curious vitality, dates from the Classic period. Its rise from minor ceremonial center to metropolitan city came relatively late and owes much to one remarkable ruler, Pacal (A.D. 603-83), and his successors, Bahlum and Kuk. These three seem to have formulated the official Palenque mythology based on a divine origin for the royal dynasty and on the supernatural passage of power from one ruler to the next.

Unlike every other Classic site, Palenque has no carved stelae. Dated inscriptions are incorporated into the bas-reliefs and the high-relief stucco decorations. Many of the motifs are strikingly similar to those found in Buddhist countries.

According to tradition, the Buddha's third week of meditation was spent under a sacred tree. It was during this time that a serpent spread his hood to shield the divine meditator from the heat of the sun. For this reason, the sun, the tree, and the serpent are three of the most sacred symbols of the Buddhist. They are equally sacred to the

Mayas. The similarities don't end here. Both Buddhists and Mayas believe that the world has been destroyed four times with a fifth destruction yet to come.

A sculpture in the Palace courtyard

Only partially redeemed from the jungle, Palenque remains a magnificent sight which rivals the sanctuary of Apollo at Delphi. Gleaming like alabaster, it lies upon the dark flanks of the Tumbala Mountains in the midst of a rain forest.

The approach is from the west. The Palace comes first into view, and then, to the right is the Temple of the Inscriptions. Various little temples lie to the east including the Temples of the Sun, the Cross, and the Foliated Cross. The North Group, a series of edifices (to the north of the Palace) includes the Temple of the Count. A pre-Columbian aqueduct directs the waters of the Otulun, a stream, to the center of the city, the only example of this kind of construction in Mayan civilization. In addition to these ruins there are literally hundreds more in the surrounding bush. The exposed part of the site is at most a half mile in extent while more ruins are known to extend for another six miles.

The **Palace** is a rectangular complex of broad stairways and numerous rooms, long corridors and a three-story tower, grouped around four large inner courtyards. This stunning building with its pagoda-like feeling contains 176 separate items of painting, stone carvings and stucco sculpture that have been called the finest examples of this ancient art in the world today. Themes of accession and death, divinity and royalty are never out of view.

This building, like so many others in Mayaland, is a kind of time machine. When the great Pacal died, it was arranged in such a way that from any vantage point in the Palace Complex, the sun at winter solstice appears to set into the earth at his tomb and the great temple constructed above it. Not only art and architecture, but the whole order of the universe were called forth to reinforce his religious and political ideology.

It used to be that no one thought that Mayan pyramids were used for tombs but that was pre-Alberto Ruz Lhuiller. One day in 1948 this Mexican archaeologist was staring at the floor of the **Temple of the Inscriptions.** The floor differed from the others by reason of its flagstones which were beautifully worked and fitted together almost perfectly. Some were particularly large. One slab had a double row of holes bored into it, so that the heavy stone could be lifted. When Lhuiller investigated, he found that the floor appeared higher in places than the bottom of the walls.

Realizing that another hidden room must lie below, he had the heavy flagstone lifted. Below was a passage blocked by sand and rocks. It took four field seasons before they reached the foot of the stairs. The concealed staircase led down into the interior of the pyramid. At the foot of the stairs the archaeologists found sacrificial offerings consisting of jade earplugs and beads, red shells and a perfect tear shaped pearl.

Another wall was removed and behind it were the skeletons of six young men. Eighty-two feet below the floor of the temple and six and a half feet below the base of the pyramid the passage ended. Or did it?

A closer scrutiny revealed that it was blocked by a triangular stone slab. On June 15, 1952 Lhuiller and his patient, hard working crew were rewarded when the last obstacle was removed and they saw before them the tomb of a Mayan king—with all its priceless array of funerary gifts—completely intact

This, they soon realized, was the tomb of Pacal himself. The great ruler and the attendants who'd accompanied him on his journey into the after-life, were buried with a splendor unique in the entire Mayan civilization.

The tomb chamber itself was a large vaulted room containing nine great figures in stucco relief, slightly larger than life-size, forming a procession around the walls. In the center lay a sarcophagus with a huge elaborately carved stone lid. The skeleton inside was lavishly arrayed with jade jewelry which included a headdress, a necklace of beads in many forms, and elaborate, delicately incised jade earplugs.

At the time of burial Pacal, had been wearing a jade mosaic mask with inlaid eyes of shell and obsidian. In his hands he held great jade beads and in his mouth was another jade bead. Even more jade objects were twined about his feet. Red cinnabar had been sprinkled over the body, the jade ornaments and the interior sides of the sarcophagus. The color red was associated with the east and the rising sun and may have been symbolic of rebirth.

Today the treasures repose at the National Museum of Archaeology in Mexico City, but one can still descend into the tomb. Many find the covering of the sarcophagus particularly interesting, seeing in the intricate design the image of a man at the controls of a space ship.

Beyond this temple a narrow path leads off into the jungle. It's only a short walk to the **Temple of the Jaguar,** but once away from the sight and sound of the main cluster of buildings one finds a lost world of contemplation. The wall carving inside the temple shows a man seated with one leg in a lotus position while the other dangles from a splendid throne which is supported by the legs of a jaguar. Jaguar heads protrude from either side of the throne. The over all effect is decidedly oriental.

One of the most distant temples is possibly the most architecturally intriguing. The relief work in the **Temple of the Foliated Cross** is identical to a temple found in Angkor Wat in Cambodia. Add to this mystery the preponderance of lotus flowers in the wall designs throughout Palenque—a flower that did not exist in Mexico at the time the city was constructed. Puzzles and more puzzles. Latter day skeptics call Count de Waldeck's conclusions "fanciful," yet the striking similarities between two far distant cultures are difficult to explain away.

In this temple the constructural elements are exposed. Its layout is similar to the **Temple of the Sun** and the **Temple of the Cross** nearby. The central tryptich panel is in place depicting two priests, one tall and one short, worshipping a central figure thought to be a stylized version of the all important maize god.

The **Temple of the Count** still contains some excellent hieroglyphic panels by the central doorway. Inside the temple, three graves were discovered in a row, all sealed with slabs and lime. Upon investigation, each grave was found to contain a cache of rich funerary objects but no human remains.

It's easy to understand how the Count de Waldeck came to select his "house," angled as it is in a manner that provides both natural air conditioning and a breathtaking view of the entire site. A fresh mountain stream flows close by; beyond it, ruins glisten like jewels against emerald velvet.

It's fun to sit on the count's front steps, alabaster stairs leading to his temple hideaway, and try to imagine the daily life of that amazing man and his woman friend. Perhaps this is where they sat at day's end watching the sun turn the old stones to burnished gold. Maybe while he sketched, she regaled him with local legends. It's possible that he offered her cognac; more likely, she introduced him to *balche*.

All we can know today is that they lived here together for two years . When Count Waldeck returned to Europe it was because he was gravely ill and may well have thought he was dying; but once back in Europe he made an amazing recovery. There were more adventures, amorous and otherwise. The count decided he was ready for marriage at 102.   He died five years later in Paris, struck by a passing carriage as he paused to admire a pretty young woman.

GETTING THERE

The easiest way to reach Palenque is to fly into Villahermosa (a lively boomtown with a fabulous museum park filled with Olmec treasures).   From here, you can catch a bus or rent a car. Palenque is less than an hour's drive on a good road.   Once there, a car's not essential. Colectivos, little minibuses or vans, shuttle back and forth between town and ruins every 15 or 20 minutes literally for pennies.

The ruins are open from 8 to 5 daily, the price is nominal. If possible, go first thing in the morning, then return toward late afternoon.   Or go for the whole day and take your bathing suit. There's a hidden pool near the tiny museum.

WHERE TO STAY & EAT

Chan-kah is the most elegant hotel. Attractive, well furnished bungalows look out at exotic gardens.   There's also a pleasant dining room on the premises.

Motel Nututum is the most atmospheric. The setting–right on the Rio Tulija–is beautiful. It's refreshing to take a dip here in the cool river water after a day of clambering up and down pyramids.   The palm thatched dining room serves excellent food and looks out over the river.

Mision Palenque—a modern hotel with a country club

atmosphere and a sociable monkey offers a convenient shuttle service to and from the ruins.

All these hotels, plus **Hotel La Canada,** on the edge of town, fall well within the reasonable category. Close by Hotel La Canada, on Calle Merle Green, is **La Selva,** the town's best restaurant. The food is consistently good here and excellent live music is a frequent dividend.

Kneeling Maya – Palenque

A mural at Bonampak

Bonampak
(bow-nam-pawk)

"The figures depicted on these extraordinary paintings—the equals of any to be found in Crete, China or India—radiate aggression. Intellectual the Mayas most certainly were, but they were also just as implacable, just as ruthless, just as savage, just as human as any of the other tribes of the western hemisphere. Here at last was the full interplay of life forces only hinted at by the sculptured monuments of other Mayan cities."

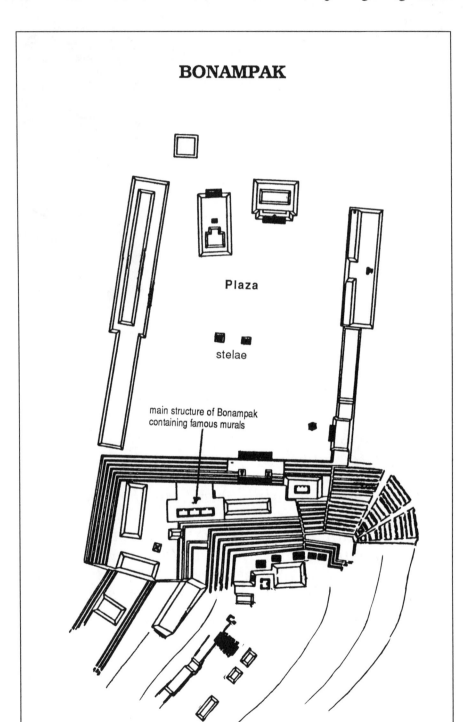

BONAMPAK

Plaza

stelae

main structure of Bonampak
containing famous murals

T he jungle trail seemed to go on forever, aimless, constricted, morning steam rising from compacted vegetation. I paused, pushed back my straw hat and thought of Saturday matinees. Tarzan. King Solomon's Mines. Green Mansions. The African Queen.

Indiana Jones, where *are* you? I wondered. Didn't he know that it was *me* out here?

This was the stuff of daydreams surely, but I was too weary to indulge myself. The guide had disappeared around the bend and I hurried on, realizing that Bonampak was still a long way away.

It was a rough trail over grown with roots. Once I stumbled and found myself at eye level with a caravan of leaf cutters each carrying a parasol of green. Above me tiny monkeys no bigger than fists pirouetted, chattering derisively at my clumsy intrusion. Shafts of light pierced the canopy of trees as high as redwoods. Here and there a toucan with a banana yellow beak beat through the still leaves. The branches that closed in about me seemed black against the filtered sunlight.

The two ornithologists in our small party seemed to spend most of their time walking with their necks thrown back, heads cocked straight up, field glasses at the ready. They spotted numerous eagles, but it was I who pointed out the sacred quetzel bird—a flash of living jade.

I pushed on, and on and on, trying hard to keep pace with the others. For me, it was a kind of endurance test, every step an effort. Then suddenly dead ahead, an improbable looking tower of massive stones appeared. Emerging from a *chicle* forest of potential chewing gum, I confronted the incredible city of Bonampak.

This is more or less what must have happened in early 1946 when a group of *chicleteros* stumbled on the ruins by accident. Hearing their stories of a city with "painted walls," photographer Giles G. Healy prevailed on the United Fruit Company to mount a mini expedition. He reached the site on May 21, 1946.

The first thing that Healy discovered was that the city wasn't really "lost" at all. The Lacandon Mayas had known of its existence for centuries and were still using the ceremonial center as a place of worship. God pots, censors and copal placed before the numerous altars bore mute testimony to recent devotions.

Healy photographed all the standing buildings except one, which he didn't see because of the dense vegetation even though it was at the very heart of the site. Later that same year when the building was discovered, it literally made history.

Up until this time, the Mayas had been considered not only the intellectuals of the new world but its pacifists. It had

been pleasant to imagine them living in splendid isolation in their remote jungle retreats peacefully star gazing or working on their complicated calendric system oblivious or possibly immune to war.

One look inside the remaining building blew that notion forever. The walls and ceilings

Rendition from the Bonampak murals

of the three inner rooms were covered with murals. The figures depicted on these extraordinary paintings—the equals of any to be found in Crete, China or India–radiate aggression.   Intellectual the Mayas most certainly were, but they were also just as implacable, just as ruthless, just as savage, just as human as any of the other tribes of the western hemisphere. Here at last was the full interplay of life forces only hinted at by the sculptured monuments of other Mayan cities.

Taken together these three rooms form a continuous narrative depicting a raid on enemy territory, a counsel of victorious chiefs, the judgment of prisoners, and finally a sacrificial ceremony and victory celebration.

Figures are close to life-size and possess a remarkable sense of motion only momentarily arrested. The colors– vibrant reds, greens and yellows, a black that seems to shine against a backdrop of the famous Mayan blue–are spectacular.

This was a classic fresco in which cement was applied to the walls and the original drawing executed immediately before they could dry. Then the artist's assistants–and there must have been many–applied the colors. It's believed by the muralist who copied the work for the Museum of Anthropology in Mexico City that the entire mural was completed in forty-eight hours, a continuous effort of artists and plasterers working simultaneously. The result has been compared to the Sistine Chapel.

The 270 figures are rendered with remarkable naturalism, some characters discernible in more than one scene.   The sacrificial victims show anguish, the battle scenes bristle with sound and fury, the presiding lord and his lady are so regal in their style and bearing, so realistic in their arrogance that one expects at any moment to see a cool nod of dismissal.

But remarkable as these murals are as artforms, the statement they make about the Mayas is of far greater significance. Here is a kind of true confession. The marauding warriors attacking nude, defenseless farmers depicted on the walls of Bonampak are a far cry from the mellow star gazers of earlier conjecture. The treatment of the captives pictured on the temple walls belies the theory that ritual sacrifice was forced on the Mayas by Toltec invaders.   This revolutionary discovery altered the whole concept of Mayan society.   After more than forty years, literature is only just beginning to come to terms with this change.

In their book, *The Blood of Kings: Dynasty and Ritual in Maya Art*, (Kimbell Art Museum, Fort. Worth, Texas, 1986), art historians Linda Schele and Mary Ellen Miller wrote, "Blood was the mortar of ancient Maya ritual life. Rulers were viewed as descendants of the gods. It was considered their duty to bleed and mutilate themselves on ritual occasions (a scene depicted in the murals) to cement their divine lineage and sustain the universe. Before going to war, for example, a king would puncture his penis with a stingray spine or a lancet made of jade or obsidian, while his queen would run a thorn-encrusted rope through her tongue. The trauma of massive blood loss induced hallucinations in which royalty contacted the gods and dead ancestors."

Though exposure to light since their discovery has caused the murals to fade, they remain one of the world's great art treasures; and one can see an excellent reproduction of their original glory at the Anthropology Museum in Mexico City.

At the foot of the terraced hill below the temple is an enormous stela celebrating the warrior king of the murals, Jalach Huinic. He holds a spear in his right hand and a religious mask in his left. Two representations of the maize god adorn the lowers sides of this carved stone.

The rest of the site is interesting, a remote jungle outpost with a variety of tumbling temples covered with curious red moss, stone idols wearing spring bonnets of orchids, and stelae which tell chilling stories of blood sacrifice. Bonampak can be reached by bush plane from San Cristobal; or, as I did, by making arrangements in Palenque to go by Land-rover to a remote Lacandon village.

SIDE TRIP to a remote Lacandon village

The side trip is a four hour journey over rough roads. From there it's a five-mile walk into the jungle (and another five back out.) An excellent dinner of venison, tortillas, beans and beer was served in the village where we spent the night. It was a choice of hammocks or pup tents. The ground was hard without padding (I opted for the tent) and the night cold. It wasn't an easy experience, but I wouldn't have missed it.

The Lancandon Mayas are a splinter group, descended from rebels who fled the conquistadores more than 400 years ago taking refuge deep in the jungle —where they still live. The Christian Mayas in Yucatan call their heathen cousins "gentiles." The Lacandons ignore the distinction. The Yucatecs, they say, merely have "different saints."

A visit to a Lacandon village is a journey into another time. The compound where I stayed was made up of five *chosas* , palm-thatched roofs supported by poles but without sides. The largest one was the kitchen, the others were used for sleeping.

Life is primitive. The men still hunt with bows and arrows, the arrows tipped with parrot feathers. The women grind corn on stone *metates* and weave cloth on small back-strap, horizontal looms. The concept of unisex would be nothing new to these people. Both men and women wear only one garment, a loose, white, knee-length gown which hangs about the ankles. Men, women and children all wear their hair shoulder length, making gender determination difficult for a stranger.

Obviously they know who's who, for this is a strongly patri-archal society. It's the man's responsibility to propitiate the gods. One means of doing this is to feed them. Before the family begins to eat, the male head of the household places food and an occasional cigar before the statues of the family gods. This ritual is not simply a prelude to a particular meal, but a means of sustaining the gods so that they can continue to provide food for the family.

The Lancandon Mayas pay homage to their gods with incense as well as food. After a time the "dead" incense burners are taken to a special burial ground when obsequities are transferred to new ones–just as Hindus do with their images when a term of service is over.

Approach to Bonampak

Entrance to labyrinth

Yaxchilan

(yash-ee-lawn)

"Yaxchilan has yet to be excavated. The Mexican Government guards the site's virginity carefully. No one goes far without a guide, though it's hard to imagine anyone wanting to. The jungle with its indefinable scent of ferns, leaf mold and green life is particularly dense here. Getting lost could be fatal."

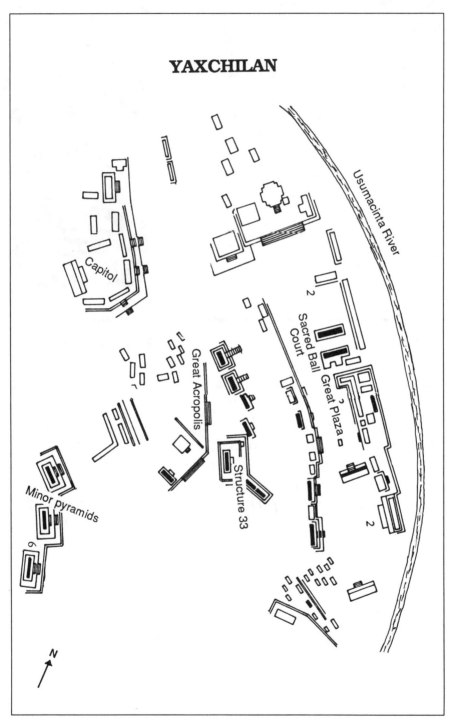

YAXCHILAN

Usumacinta River

Capitol

Sacred Ball Court

Great Plaza

Great Acropolis

Structure 33

Minor pyramids

N

I f, as they say, "the road to Rome *is* Rome," then most certainly the road to Yaxchilan is Yaxchilan. Whether you fly in by bush plane or travel as I did by dugout canoe, the journey is a grand adventure.

The mighty Usamacinta River which divides Mexico from Guatemala is flanked on either side by the largest surviving rain forest in Northern America. Giant mahogany trees rising as high as 150 feet and sacred ceibas with tall straight trunks leafed at the top like umbrellas are silent sentinels guarding the banks. Orchids grow everywhere, begonias are waist high. This is truly the forest primeval.

A long, mahogany dugout with an outboard motor had taken me down river. Aided by the current it took just under three hours, a triumph of white water navigational skill. Varying depths and a jagged, uneven bottom make for dangerous pulsing currents and boiling rapids. There were exciting glimpses of bands of wild monkeys, of toucans and eagles. I watched for alligators—remembering that earlier explorers had written of hearing their teeth chomping at night. I didn't see any. Nor did I spot any Guatemalan guerrillas, though our progress was surely monitored from their side of the river. The Usumacinta traverses a tangled region, ecologically and politically. Aggressive Marxist forces have found the remoteness well suited to their survival. For centuries the name has been synonymous with trackless impenetrability.

At last the dugout headed for a sandy spit. Just above it was a small compound where the caretaker lives. Only a few yards beyond the jungle begins. Beyond that lies Yaxchilan, the "lost" city of my dreams.

G

Yaxchilan has yet to be excavated. The Mexican Government guards the site's virginity carefully. No one goes far

without a guide, though it's hard to imagine anyone wanting to. The jungle with its indefinable scent of ferns, leaf
mold and green life is particularly dense here. Getting lost
could be fatal.

Despite the almost daily efforts of caretakers to keep the
bush at bay, Yaxchilan lies uneasily before the jungle jug-
gernaut. Tree-size roots extending down through roofs,
walls and subterranean chambers, tear apart massive
stones. Strangler vines creep over balustrades, through
corbelled arches, binding statues of Chac, enshrouding figures of dead monarchs in leafy winding sheets.

Believed to have been a city of seers, Yaxchilan remains a
place of brooding mystery. A narrow, rocky path leads
through the jungle past the small airstrip emerging before
two crumbling pyramids. Four pitch black entrances in the
second structure lead into a labyrinth. The purpose of these
inter-connecting chambers is unknown.

What we *do* know about Yaxchilan is that it was built during the Mayan Golden Age, 200-900 AD, and reached its apogee during the 8th century under the governorship of Jaguar Shield and his son, Bird Jaguar. Their signatures are
prominently placed throughout the site. (Jaguar Shield depicted by a jaguar profile, his son a slightly smaller jaguar
with quetzal feathers exploding from his forehead.)

Emerging from the labyrinth, you're confronted by the grim
specter of sacrificial stones and the grand vista of the central courtyard. The topography of Yaxchilan's riverside location ruled out the strict geometric configurations that
characterize most Mayan ceremonial centers. The effect
here is more organic than monumental.

There are eighty-six known structures. Some are located

on the hill near the river, others are found on still higher el-
evations. The labyrinth remains the most intriguing. Even
today the Mayas regard caves as entrances to the underworld and avenues of communication with the gods. During Yaxchilan's heyday this must certainly have been the
heart of the peoples' religious devotions, magic rituals and
secrets.

This is a ceremonial center filled with mystical symbolism.
A reoccurring artistic theme throughout is one of blood let-
ting–known to have induced altered states of conscious-
ness. (A similar practice is still employed by the Hindu de-
votees of the deity Kali.) Near the labyrinth is the **Jaguar
Temple** where one can see a carving of Jaguar Shield sitting in an eternal lotus position. Another remarkable stela
depicts a woman serving a serpent, the serpent is thought
to represent the beginning of new life.

Structure 33, considered by some to be the most interesting
temple at Yaxchilan, is situated on a small rise overlooking
the main plaza. Before the doorway is a headless statue of a
humanized feline figure in a posture of worship. Many
years ago mahogany cutters broke off the head- which can
be seen a few feet away.

Lancandon Mayas still frequent this holy city of their ancient culture burning copal and offering prayers to the time
when the head and body will be reunited. They believe the
sacred union will mark the destruction of this world and
the beginning of a new one signaling the rebirth of the old
gods and the final flowering of the ancient Maya culture.

Sitting in the central plaza of this forgotten city of seers almost anything seems possible. The angry roar of howler
monkeys punctuates the incessant hum of cicadas. It's a
long, long way from anywhere.

Agua Azul – a side trip out of Palenque

Appendix

*"The best way to enjoy
Mexican food is simply to relax."*

Xel-ha

WHAT TO DO UNTIL THE CURANDERO COMES

Turista isn't inevitable. After 18 trips to Mexico, I've yet to experience it—though I've gotten "ze trots" twice in France.

A government seeking tourists is going to do everything in its power to keep them carefree and comfortable. Many Mexican hotels and restaurants have their own water purification systems. As a travel writer I've inspected many. The possibility of picking up the nasty E. Coli bacteria in such pristine places is probably less than in your kitchen or mine. Of course, if you plan to venture off the tourist circuit, the odds change. Though Mexico often seems like an exotic annex to California, it's still a Third World country with a few potential hazards.

The best way to avoid the need for a *curandero* or healer is to practice preventative medicine. The day before leaving for Mexico, I zap my immune system with a gamma globulin shot. This virtually guarantees immunity to Hepatitis A which is transmitted the same way as travelers diarrhea, via water and food that's been contaminated with sewage. A common source of hepatitis A is eating raw shellfish that was caught in polluted water. In other words, you can get it at home as easy or easier than in Mexico.

Though developed primarily for hepatitis A, gamma globulin seems to strengthen the body's resistance in other, as yet, undefined ways. In addition to this shot, I take a sulfatrim tablet on the day I leave and on every day of my trip. This combination continues to sustain me in some highly primitive areas.

Whenever possible I drink bottled water, beer, soft drinks, etc. I also purify my own drinking water by dissolving halizone tablets in the carafes left in my hotel room. I carry this water with me in a plastic flask and also brush my teeth with it. Besides halizone, my medicine bag contains Pepto Bismol tablets–just in case.

Friends who prefer to " wait and see" rather than take medication before the fact swear by lomotil. Lomotil is available at any farmacia in Mexico without a prescription, as are two other standbys: streptomagnum and mexaform. However, since each of us reacts differently to medication, it's a good idea to check with your doctor.

GETTING AROUND

Planes–Mexicana flies to Cancun from Baltimore, Chicago, Dallas, Denver, Los Angeles, Miami, Philadelphia, San Antonio, and Mexico City with connecting service to Merida and Villahermosa.   Aeromexico has departures from Houston, New York, Los Angeles and Mexico City. United, Continental and American also serve Cancun.

Trains–There's very little that I can say about taking trains on the Yucatan Peninsula other than **don't**. At one time there was an excellent sleeper car that left Merida around midnight and reached Palenque the next morning. Unfortunately, this service was discontinued in early 1987. Yes, there's still a night train. I was told the trip would take 12 hours. In reality, it was 17.

Yes, it was an opportunity to experience the *real* Mexico: snoring passengers, wailing babies, loud music, etc. There are other, easier ways. Besides being a long, hard trip, it can also be dangerous. I've known people who've been robbed.

Buses–the bus system in Mexico is relatively efficient and seems to go everywhere. This really is a good way to meet all kinds of people. If you're traveling light, are in reasonably good physical condition, possess a sense of humor and an adaptable nature, traveling by bus can be fun. Sometimes bus seats can be reserved, try to arrange this whenever possible. Check and re-check everything.

Car–there are two very different kinds of people who don't like traveling by car in Mexico. One kind feels that car travel tends to "isolate" them from the real Mexico. In a way, it does; but after my numerous bus and train experiences, I find there's something to be said for isolation.

The other kind of person avoids car travel out of fear. There's always somebody who knows somebody who heard this horror story from someone else. As far as I'm concerned, driving a car in Mexico is no different from driving one anywhere.

Whether you drive your own car or rent one, insurance is essential. Rental cars are highly competitive, so do comparison shop. When you leave town be sure that you have a full tank of gas. Service stations aren't as prevalent in Mexico as they are in the United States. Roads in Yucatan, Quintana Roo and most of Chiapas are excellent, but I don't suggest night driving in remote areas. (I wouldn't suggest it in remote areas of the United States either.)

Recently a car I'd rented broke down in the middle of a tiny village–fortunately in broad day light. People emerged out of nowhere and pushed the car over to the side. There were offers to help, but the car appeared beyond help. There was no phone, but a bus came by. My companion hopped on and the driver detoured to take him to the very door of a garage.

I waited with the car practicing my Spanish on the children who appeared out of nowhere to admire my red fingernails and jewelry. By the time my friend returned with the mechanic I'd met all twenty residents of the town. Before long the car was drivable and we were on our way, but the next day as we were about to leave Valladolid it acted up again.

This time we called the rental office in Cancun. Within two hours a representative was there with a new car. All repair connected bills were matter of factly subtracted from the final rental fee when we turned in the second car at the Merida airport. I've had cars breakdown in Lisbon, on the island of Crete and the Hollywood freeway. It can happen anywhere.

That relatively remote possibility is scarcely worth the loss of mobility and independence that car travel offers.

MAYA MEALS

The best way to enjoy Mexican food is simply to relax. Speed is not a quality on which Mexican waiters pride themselves. Additionally, they consider it tacky to present the bill without being asked for it. This lifestyle offers a splendid behavior modification opportunity for Type A's.

Forget who you are and where you came from and think instead about the reasons why you needed this vacation. While you're contemplating, you can also practice a little Spanish. *La cuenta, por favor* (the bill, please) for instance.

Separated from most of Mexico by water and jungle, the Yucatan Peninsula has a character all its own. The early colonists had far more in common with Europe and Cuba than they had with Mexico. This and the Mayan influence accounts for the area's independent spirit and unique cuisine.

The *frijol negro*, a rich black bean, is popular throughout Yucatan as well as in the Caribbean islands. Banana leaves are used for wrapping tamales, meats, and fowl while steaming, baking, and grilling--open-fire cooking is common in Yucatan. The bitter Seville orange and sour lime are peculiar to the peninsula, adding a tangy touch to sauced dishes.

The Yucatan has several specialties which you'll see often on menus. Once away from Cancun, the English explanations will be omitted. A few to remember are:

Sopa de Lima-chicken broth, lime juice, onion, corn, chips and small pieces of chicken.

Cochinita Pibil-baked pig with sour orange juice, salt, and banana leaves served with relish made of onion, coriander leaves, hot pepper and salt.

Sac-kol de Jambali-Wild boar with sauce made of corn flour, tomato and peppermints leaves.

Pok-chuc-broiled pork meat, tomato, onion, coriander leaves and sour orange served with black beans.

Tzic de Venado-baked venison, shredded and mixed with coriander leaves, radish, mint leaves and sour orange juice.

Pavo en Relleno Negro-turkey with tomato, achiote, epazote, salt, vinegar, hot peppers and pork meat stuffing.

other travel & travel related books from

Wide World Publishing/Tetra

P.O. Box 476 • San Carlos, CA 94070

HAWAII–*Island Paradise*

An artistic representation of the Hawaiian experience • Illustrations are paired with quotations from Mark Twain, Jack London, Isabella Bird, John La Farge, Pegge Hopper and others. This book is a collection of impressions by a variety of visitors to the island paradise of Hawaii. Helps rekindle the memories of multihued skies, the fragrance of plumeria blossoms and the caresses of the tradewinds. Evokes the mood of aloha!　　　•156 pages•illustrations•81/2"x11"
•ISBN:0-9331742-42-X•$9.95

HAWAII
Island Paradise

A Guide to PLACES OF WORSHIP — *In and Around San Francisco*
by Elvira Monroe
A *non-secular* guide to the art, history and architecture of 32 churches, synagogues, temples, missions, cathedrals and chapels in and around San Francisco.
"An example of how good a local guide can be." — **San Francisco Chronicle**
　•188 pages • maps, diagrams, b/w photos•51/2"x81/2" • ISBN: 0-933174-24-1 • $6.95

GREEK COOKING FOR EVERYONE
by Theoni Pappas & Elvira Monroe
The extensive and authentic recipes are arranged by menus for 22 complete dinners. This format helps take the guesswork out of deciding what to serve with what. Special sections on desserts, breads, wines, coffee, cheeses, herbs and delicacies from the vendors.
" Stirs Greek spirit and captures the essense of Greek cooking ... a good gift for non-Greek cooks as well as those who collect Greek recipes. —
Hellenic Journal
　• 167 pages with 66 B/Wphotos of Greece
•ISBN: 0-933174-29-2• $7.95

HAWAII–Cooking with Aloha
by Elvira Monroe & Irish Margah
This book will help recreate the wonder and moods of a vacation in Hawaii's tropical paradise. 130 recipes include countless pupus•main dishes ranging from Kalua pig to curries•side dishes such as Portugese bean soup, lomi salmon and baked bananas •salads•breads•beverages. Special desserts include Mai Tai Pie, Kona Coffee Ice Cream Pie, Macadamia Nut Pie, Papaya Chiffon and Pineapple cheesecakes. Menus for a luau, dinner, suppers, barbeques and brunches are an added feature. Further enchancing the book are hints on decor, information on various islands and guidelines on selecting papayas, avocadoes and pineapples. Relive the magic of the tradewinds, swaying palms, white sands and the blue sky and sea.

•199 pages with illustrations
•Over 130 recipes•ISBN: 0-933174-22-5•$7.95

Available from your local bookstore or directly from
WIde World Publishing/Tetra, postage prepaid.

ABOUT THE AUTHOR

A writer who has traveled extensively all over the world, Antoinette May is repeatedly drawn to Mexico. As a psychic researcher whose work has been the subject of such TV documentaries as *In Search Of* and *The World of People,* she's particularly intrigued by the dark mysteries of this remarkable land.

May is a biographer, a former newspaper editor, and the founder and publisher of a women's magazine. She writes a weekly column for the San Francisco *Chronicle* and lectures on parapsychology at universities and colleges.

Other books by Antoinette May •*Witness to War*
• *Helen Hunt Jackson: A Lonely Voice of Conscience*
• *Psychic Women* • *Free Spirit, Different Drummers*
• *Haunted Houses and Wandering Ghosts of California*

Antoinette May at Chichen Itza